GIVES ME HOPE

The 127 Most Inspiring Bite-Sized Stories

# GIVES ME HOPE

## The 127 Most Inspiring Bite-Sized Stories

edited by

EMERSON SPARTZ and GABY SPARTZ

Ulysses Press

Published by: Ulysses Press
P.O. Box 3440
Berkeley, CA 94703
www.ulyssespress.com

ISBN: 978-1-56975-828-1
Library of Congress Catalog Number 2010935013

Printed in Canada by Transcontinental Printing

10 9 8 7 6 5 4 3 2 1

Acquisitions Editor: Keith Riegert
Managing Editor: Claire Chun
Proofreader: Elyce Petker
Production: Judith Metzener
Cover design: Dylan Spartz
Interior photos: see page 151

Distributed by Publishers Group West

Thousands of candles can be lit from a single candle,
and the life of the candle will not be shortened.
Happiness never decreases by being shared.

*Siddhartha Gautama*

# GivesMeHope:
# Inspiration in a World of Negativity

Like it or not, we live in a media-driven world where negative news clutters the airwaves. As they say in journalism, "If it bleeds, it leads." Naturally, our interest is piqued by the shock of murders, robberies, accidents, kidnappings, and violence. But without limit, this negativity takes a toll on our collective psyche.

We are exhausted by the mainstream media's fixation on the dark side. We are tired of hearing what's wrong in this world. That is why we created GivesMeHope.

We believe that for every negative story in the world, there is an inspiring story about something great happening to someone. We believe there should be a place for people to share those stories.

GivesMeHope is that place.

On GivesMeHope.com, people share with the world their most hopeful, uplifting moments—stories of amazing friends, everlasting love, and random acts of kindness.

We launched the site in 2009, cautiously optimistic of its reception. Would people be interested? Or was the siren call of gore and gossip just too strong?

The response was overwhelming. The website quickly generated media attention and received over 100,000 unique visitors in its very first day! By providing a home for people to share their inspirational stories, GivesMeHope has become a source of strength for millions of people. The stories have inspired students to stay in school, saved troubled marriages, helped girls and boys with body-image issues, and have even brought readers back from the verge of suicide. One such reader remarked that he "could never leave a world that contain[s] such beauty."

This book, *GivesMeHope: The 127 Most Inspiring Bite-Sized Stories*, is a combination of old favorites from the website and brand new, never-before-seen stories—all told artfully through powerful, full-color imagery.

Our day-to-day struggles often cause us to lose sight of the beauty in the world. GivesMeHope reminds us to appreciate that beauty. We hope reading these stories is as inspiring for you as it has been for us.

EMERSON SPARTZ and GABY SPARTZ
Creators of GivesMeHope.com

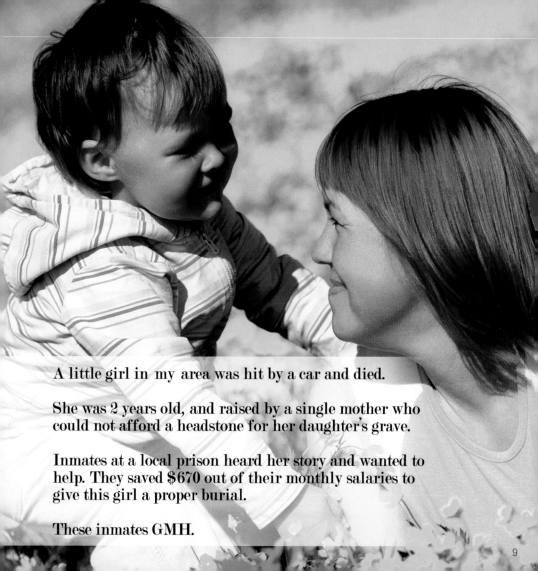

A little girl in my area was hit by a car and died.

She was 2 years old, and raised by a single mother who could not afford a headstone for her daughter's grave.

Inmates at a local prison heard her story and wanted to help. They saved $670 out of their monthly salaries to give this girl a proper burial.

These inmates GMH.

there's a friendly homeless man who always rides the same subway, selling trinkets for 25 cents each, usually to buy food.

today, instead of collecting the money for himself, he was sending his proceeds to help the victims in haiti.

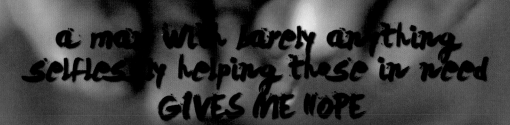

a man with barely anything selflessly helping those in need GIVES ME HOPE

22 years ago, a 16-year-old girl was pregnant with a BABY OF RAPE.

Her parents told her to *ABORT* or be *DISOWNED*.

HER BEST FRIEND - HER 18-YEAR-OLD NEIGHBOR - ALTHOUGH HE WAS NOT THE FATHER, STEPPED INTO THE FATHER FIGURE'S SHOES.

THEY GOT MARRIED 2 YEARS LATER.

MOM AND DAD, YOUR LOVE FOR ME AND FOR EACH OTHER

gmh

# LAST YEAR,

a local boat carrying various
aged passengers home,
*flipped during a storm.*

**There was a teenaged boy
and a baby aboard.
Though the teenaged boy couldn't swim,
he placed the baby
on the last floating device—
a cushion.**

The teenaged boy drowned.
He was a basketball player
and a senior in high school.

# YOUR SELFLESSNESS GMH.
# RIP RISHARD.

My friend was always depressed. One day, she attempted suicide and a guy she never really talked to at school visited her at the hospital.

He said, "Don't you dare do that again! You are the MOST beautiful girl that I have seen.

## EVER."

That was 6 years ago. They're getting married this weekend.

**5** years ago, a friend from Oklahoma and I were talking about how we hardly ever get snow in Texas. He said that he wished he could make it snow for me.

TWO YEARS LATER, **HE DIED SUDDENLY.** BY THE TIME I FOUND OUT, I HAD ALREADY MISSED THE FUNERAL.

That same day, it snowed. Then it snowed again on my birthday. In April. Knowing he's watching over me

My friend and I won toys at a fair and gave them to a mentally disabled boy. He said, "Thank you."

His father cried. <u>The boy hadn't spoken in months.</u>

**Children like him GMH.**

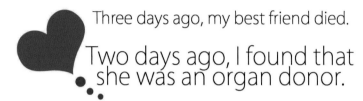

Three days ago, my best friend died.

Two days ago, I found that she was an organ donor.

One day ago, I heard that a nine-year-old boy now had her heart.

Today, I met that nine-year-old boy.
He told me that because he had my
best friend's heart, he'd be my best friend now.

My best friend and him GMH.

A girl I went to high school with was diagnosed with leukemia her junior year.

She lost all of her hair due to chemotherapy and was pretty upset about it.

**ONE DAY,** eight of her closest friends came to school with shaved heads, saying it was just hair, and who cared —

**BALD** is the new in.

**OTHER PEOPLE'S BOYFRIENDS** take them out for elaborate meals and buy them Tiffany bracelets.

my boyfriend, though, is eighteen, lives by himself, goes to school, pays rent, and has no money. Our dates are nights in with movies. When I see him going through his change jar to treat me to some chocolate, it makes me wanna cry. *his love* **GIVES ME HOPE**

A few months ago, I was at dinner with friends, and we ended up having an emotional talk (mostly about my self-esteem issues) and I cried for about half of dinner.

When I got the receipt, the stunning waitress had written something across the top:

"You're even beautiful when you cry."

19

TODAY, MY FRIEND GAVE ME A PIGGY-BACK RIDE AND RAN UP AND DOWN MY STREET WITH ME ON HIS BACK.

I WAS BORN WITH SPINA BIFIDA. HE WANTED ME TO KNOW WHAT RUNNING FELT LIKE.

GMH

Just over two years ago, my young daughter ran up to a stranger on the street, asking him to marry her.

**I was so embarrassed, but he was so sweet! He bought us both ice cream and after a while we started dating. Six months ago I got my very own proposal.**

LOVE

My daughter's bravery brought two soul mates together. Baby girl, you GMH

I was recently working at a nursery school where I saw a 3-year-old girl wearing tights on her head.

One of my colleagues told me it was because some of the children had been making fun of her bald head. She had had chemotherapy.

I later saw one young boy of about 4 go over to her, tell her she was beautiful, and remove the tights.

G M H

i secretly had a crush on my best friend for half a year.
one day, we were talking, and i said something silly. he replied, *"why are you my friend?"* jokingly, i said *"because you love me."*

## his reply?

"yup, so why are you my friend, and not my girlfriend?"

we've been together
9 months
now

While doing homework on one of the university computers, I spied a Sailor Moon manga on one of the others. It turned out to be a very large football player reading it. He told me that it was his little sister's new obsession and he wanted to be able to talk to her about it when she called.

My 12-year-old son has been **fighting cancer** for 7 years.

Yesterday, as he laid in his hospital bed, receiving chemotherapy to prepare for a bone marrow transplant, he asked me for his wallet.

He wanted to count his money to make sure he had enough to buy **Christmas gifts** for his siblings and an extra one... for toys for tots.

*My son always* **GMH.**

My freshman year of high school a sophmore girl with mental problems was elected to homecoming court as a cruel joke of some popular girls in her grade. when our senior class president found out about this, he ditched his date, who was one of the leaders of the prank. he then asked the mentally disabled girl if he could be her escort to the dance.

*CLASS PRESIDENTS*
WHO ARE
**CLASS ACTS**
*give me hope*

I had my students write a paper about who they admired most.

They had to read their papers out loud. One girl chose to write about her friend that had recently committed suicide. She started crying in the middle of reading her paper.

Two boys, one of whom was very shy, ran to the front of the class and hugged her... in front of everybody.

Boys like these GMH.

One day, while heavily pregnant with me, my mother fainted on the sidewalk. A homeless man helped her get to the hospital safely.

Out of gratitude, my parents paid for his art courses at a local art school.

On every holiday, 20 years later, he sends my daughter beautiful picture books he illustrated.

GMH.

Today, I saw my older brother for the first time in almost **five years.**

Very shocked by his long hair, I asked him if he wanted me to **cut it.**

He freaked out and said it only needed to grow two more inches before he could have a wig made for his wife of almost ten years, whose hair was beginning to fall out from cancer. His love **GMH.**

29

Today, I found out about a 10-year old boy who has been harassed by his classmates because he refuses to say the Pledge of Allegiance.

# Why?

He says that until gays and lesbians have equal rights, there isn't really "liberty and justice for all."

Kids with the courage to stand up for their fellow human beings GMH.

When I was 11 years old,
about a month before my dad passed,
he was almost completely paralyzed and the
doctors were sure he would never
be able to speak again.

Just out of the blue, he said my name.

They called me and put him on the phone,
and he said he loved me three times.

GMH

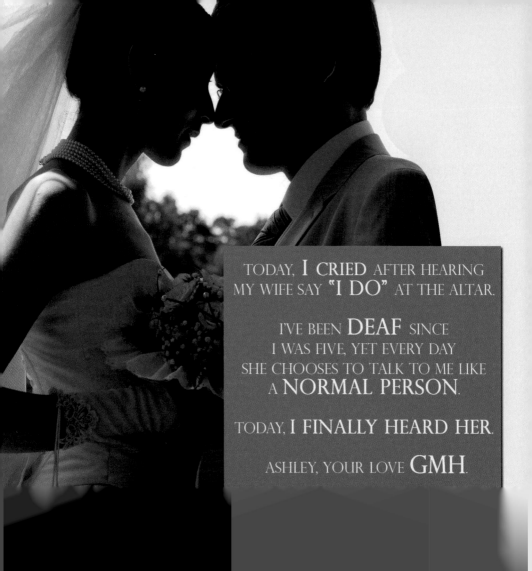

TODAY, **I CRIED** AFTER HEARING
MY WIFE SAY "**I DO**" AT THE ALTAR.

I'VE BEEN **DEAF** SINCE
I WAS FIVE, YET EVERY DAY
SHE CHOOSES TO TALK TO ME LIKE
A **NORMAL PERSON**.

TODAY, **I FINALLY HEARD HER**.

ASHLEY, YOUR LOVE **GMH**.

I'M IN LAW ENFORCEMENT, AND ONE OF MY OFFICERS TOLD ME HE ATTENDED CHURCH IN A BAD PART OF THE CITY.

HE SAID THAT DURING THE SERVICE, A DRUG DEALER CAME IN OFF OF THE STREET AND PUT ALL OF HIS DRUGS AND A GUN IN FRONT OF THE ALTAR.

HE SAID, *"Call the cops, do what you have to, I give it all up today."*

*God's love and grace gives me hope*

MY FAMILY AND I GOT SEPARATED IN NEW YORK CITY WHEN I WAS LITTLE. SCARED, I SAT CRYING ON THE SIDEWALK AS TONS OF PEOPLE PASSED BY.

A HOMELESS MAN PICKED ME UP, COMFORTED ME, AND CARRIED ME TO A POLICE OFFICER, WHO FOUND MY PARENTS.

HE HAD A LONG BEARD. I ASKED IF HE WAS JESUS.

HE LAUGHED SO HARD HE CRIED. GMH.

When I was five, my best friend and I had a fake wedding.

Today is our real one. His enduring love and friendship to this day GMH.

Several years back, I passed by an elderly man with crutches hobbling onto an interstate on-ramp. I stopped and asked the man if I could give him a ride. He said, "Yes, I'm just going to the next exit to visit my wife."

When I got to the next exit, I dropped him off at the cemetery.

His never-ending love. GMH

my sister has cancer and recently had a surgery to remove the largest tumors. But the doctors didn't remove any because it had already spread too far. they told my sister's boyfriend that it was to the terminal point.

when she woke up, he was holding a ring. he asked her to marry him.

# their love
## gives me hope

While at the store I noticed a man that was obviously mentally challenged. He wanted a free balloon that they give out to kids.

**THEY WERE OUT.**

A girl about five noticed him crying and walked up to him and said, "Here mister – you can have mine!"

The look on his face was priceless. That girl GMH.

Two years ago, I tried to kill myself by swallowing a bottle of painkillers.

My online friend — who I'd never met — was the only person who knew. He called 911, and they pumped my stomach to save my life.

Today, I got my bachelor's degree in sociology. I'm now going to graduate school.

GMH

Three years ago, I served Thanksgiving lunch to the less fortunate. Since it was during duty hours, I was still in my Air Force uniform.

After the meal, I was pushing a little girl on a swing.

When it was time to leave, she said, "Thanks for pushing me on the swing. And for saving the world."

GMH.

# Yesterday, I was watching the local news.

A story came on about a second-grader who was **diagnosed with leukemia** and lost her hair.

A boy in her class not only **shaved his head** so she wouldn't be alone, he also got the whole class to do it too.

I cried.

Good people, at all ages, GMH.

41

FIVE YEARS AGO, I WITNESSED AN OVERWEIGHT GIRL BEING HA-RASSED. A GROUP OF "POPULAR GIRLS" HAD PULLED DOWN HER PANTS WHILE WE WERE LEAVING SCHOOL. THE GIRL GRABBED HER PANTS AND RAN AWAY CRYING. OUR SCHOOL'S STAR QUARTER-BACK CHASED AFTER HER TO COMFORT HER.

I JUST CAME BACK FROM THEIR WEDDING.

GMH.

# ONE YEAR AGO, I WAS SERIOUSLY DEPRESSED AND CONTEMPLATING SUICIDE.

THE BOY WHO SAT BEHIND ME IN GEOMETRY ASKED EVERY DAY IF I WAS OKAY, DESPITE MY OFTEN *RUDE* OR *SHORT* RESPONSES. HE DIDN'T KNOW IT, BUT HIS CARING QUESTIONS WERE THE ONE THING KEEPING ME ALIVE.

*Today he is my love and my best friend. I am so much more than okay.* He GMH

My mother has raised three children by herself. Two are going to college, and one is an honors student in high school. She's been homeless several times, was raped and kept the baby, and she was disowned by every member of her family.

( She's 45 years old and attending college online with a GPA of 3.942. )

My mom GMH.

*This spring,*
I HELPED OUT
AT MY SCHOOL'S PROM
monitoring the voting
for prom queen and king.
When the winners were announced,
*they came as no surprise.*

A very popular
girl, and Shane,
who had been
surrounded by the
prettiest girls all night.

OH, BUT SHANE?
*He has down's syndrome.*

My generation GMH.

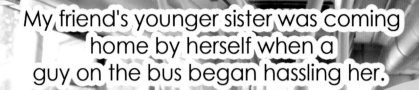

My friend's younger sister was coming home by herself when a guy on the bus began hassling her.

An elderly man on the other side of the bus stood up and demanded that the guy *"leave his granddaughter alone."*

The guy stopped, and got off at the next stop. The elderly man **was a stranger.**

Years ago I told my best friend Matt that I couldn't go to
with him because my parents couldn't afford to buy m

The night of the dance, Matt showed up at my door with a
red dress, matching shoes and corsage, and two tickets t

Three years, a marriage and one child later, he

When my grandmother was 85,
she got breast cancer.

She fought so hard and
beat it because she was
worried that my grandfather
did not know how to
use the dishwasher.

She is still alive today at 92.

Their love GMH.

Today, I found out that the police arrested my parents for abusing me.

Who's going to be my new guardian? MY 25-YEAR-OLD BROTHER, whom I haven't seen in 7 years.

He reported them, and is keeping his promise of coming back to save me.

love you, B.

YOU

M.H

Last May, I tried to kill myself. When I got home from the hospital, my family barely said a word.

I went to bed in tears, until my little brother woke me up and dragged me onto our garage roof.

He sat and watched the stars with me for two hours, telling me he loved me, and that he wants to make everything better.

My nine-year-old brother

GMH

Gives Me Hope

**at a fireworks display tonight, a man with down's syndrome sat next to me on my blanket.**

his elderly parents were next to us and started to scold him and apologize, but i said i had plenty of room. he held my hand and told me he wanted to watch fireworks with me because i was pretty and he wanted to be my friend.

**HE GIVES ME HOPE**

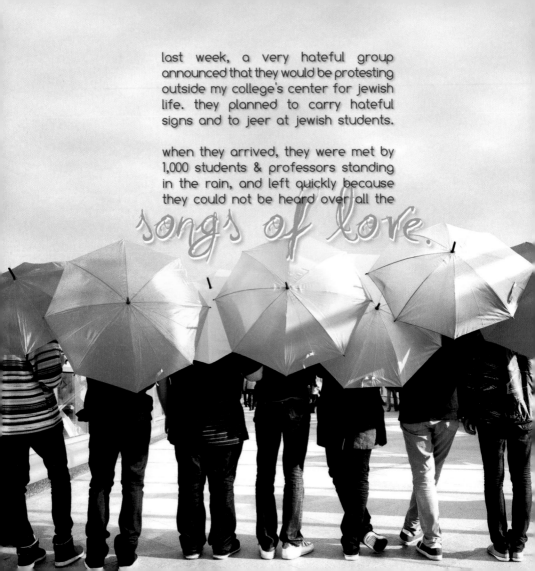

last week, a very hateful group announced that they would be protesting outside my college's center for jewish life. they planned to carry hateful signs and to jeer at jewish students.

when they arrived, they were met by 1,000 students & professors standing in the rain, and left quickly because they could not be heard over all the *songs of love.*

A FEW MONTHS AGO,
MY GRANDMOTHER DIED OF CANCER.

WITH THE FEW
WORDS SHE HAD
LEFT, SHE TOLD ME
WHERE TO FIND
MY CHRISTMAS
PRESENTS FOR THE
NEXT THREE YEARS,
MY HIGH SCHOOL
GRADUATION
PRESENT, AND MY
WEDDING PRESENT.

AS HER YOUNGEST
GRANDCHILD, SHE
WANTED TO MAKE
SURE SHE COULD BE
THERE FOR ME

EVEN
AFTER
SHE WAS
GONE

HER LOVE AND
THOUGHTFULNESS
GIVES ME HOPE

# I'm dying of lupus at age 17.

I was brought home from the hospital to have my last week.
I've been an avid Harry Potter fan for many years,
and my mother is **desperately** trying to find a way for **me** to see
the new Harry Potter theme park.

*Little does she know, her love through all of this is far better than a day in Hogsmeade.*

*She GMH*

TODAY I WAS AT THE GROCERY STORE WITH MY MOM.

AS WE WERE PUSHING OUR CART, I HEARD
A WOMAN **SOBBING.** I TURNED AROUND.

THERE STOOD A COUPLE,
LINKED ARM IN ARM,
THE WOMAN **LAUGHING**
SO HARD SHE WAS **CRYING.**

THE MAN HAD TWO CARROTS
STUFFED UP HIS NOSE,
AND HE WAS LAUGHING AS WELL.

THEY WERE ABOUT
**80 YEARS OLD.**

THEIR LOVE **GMH.**

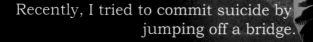

Recently, I tried to commit suicide by
jumping off a bridge.

My boyfriend saved me by jumping in
after me and pulling me out.

When I woke up in the hospital he was in a
hospital bed next to mine as he had suffered a
minor concussion.

He looked at me, smiled, and said,
"I promised I'd always catch you."

His unconditional love GMH.

We have a tradition in my church that
the men sing their wives a song on Mother's Day.

After they went up to start singing,
a man with disabilities came.

While he wasn't singing like everyone else,
I could tell from the swaying of his head
and the random sounds from his mouth
that he loved the woman he was singing to.

True love with no limits GMH.

A 5-year-old boy was crossing the street and a **drunk driver** happened to be driving down the road at the same time.

Noticing that the vehicle was not coming to a stop, a man jumped in front of the vehicle, **pushing the young boy to safety.**

He gave up his life for someone he had never met before.

He is a hero.

I miss you so much, Dad. You GMH.

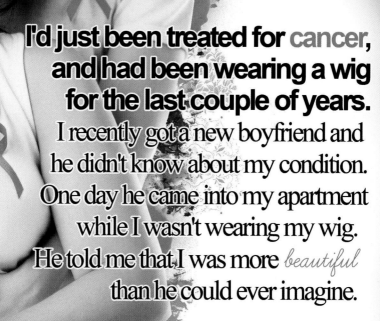

**I'd just been treated for cancer, and had been wearing a wig for the last couple of years.** I recently got a new boyfriend and he didn't know about my condition. One day he came into my apartment while I wasn't wearing my wig. He told me that I was more *beautiful* than he could ever imagine.

*He truly*

GMH

59

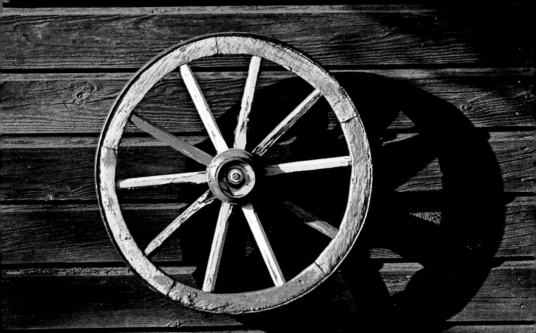

When I was 13, a bunch of girls decided to lock me into the gardening house. Little did they know the sprinklers poured down, drowning me, leaving me scared, wet and crying.

A boy punched through the glass and carried me to the school nurse, even with a bleeding, broken hand.

My now-husband's courage GMH.

Last year, my boyfriend passed away.

On my birthday, his parents gave me a memorial ring and told me that they considered me their daughter and unofficially adopted me.

His dad said, "I'm not kidding, even twenty years from now we want to be a part of your life."

They GMH.

in our school, each student has to make a report in front of the class about someone they admire. my friend reported on a quiet girl in class, admiring her kindness. we all cheered in agreement.

# the girl was crying.

LATER, I FOUND OUT THAT WAS THE DAY SHE'D DECIDED **NOT TO KILL HERSELF.**

I WOKE UP ONE MORNING TO HEAR
THE BIRDS OUTSIDE MY WINDOW AND
MY MOTHER COOKING BREAKFAST DOWNSTAIRS.

I've never cried so much in my entire life.
I HAD BEEN DEAF SINCE THE AGE OF 8.

Today, the pastor of my church anounced that his 19-year-old daughter was pregnant out of wedlock. As the pastor's wife began to cry, a little boy ran up to her and hugged her saying,

IT'S OKAY! BABIES ARE THE BEST THING IN THE WORLD, NO MATTER WHAT.

Today, three of my closest
guy friends came to
visit me in the hospital.

*Not too long ago I was
diagnosed with cancer and
I had lost all of my hair.*

They came in with flowers,
shaved heads, a smile,
and said,

**"You're beautiful to us,
even if you don't think so.
We're in this together."**

THE JANITOR AT OUR SMALL SCHOOL
HAS BEEN GOING TO HIGH SCHOOL ONLINE
FOR THE PAST FEW YEARS SINCE
HE DROPPED OUT WHEN HE WAS YOUNG.

DURING GRADUATION LAST YEAR,
BENNY WALKED ACROSS THE STAGE
WITH ALL THE SENIORS.

HE IS NEARLY 80 YEARS OLD.

FINISHING WHAT HE STARTED gmh

My senior year, I was the only girl in one of my classes and was always teased by the boys for it.

I still baked for every one of them on their birthday, expecting nothing back.

My birthday was the last in the class. I walked in that day to 17 boys holding plates of cookies.

They each baked for me, WITHOUT talking to eachother about it.

Those boys gmh

# FRESHMAN YEAR, there was a crippled girl bound to a wheelchair.

For 4 years, she did physical therapy and progressed to crutches.

When we graduated a few weeks ago,
she handed her crutches to an officer and walked across the entire stage.

THE APPLAUSE FROM THE SENIORS WAS DEAFENING.
SHE CRIED THE WHOLE WAY.

*gmh.*

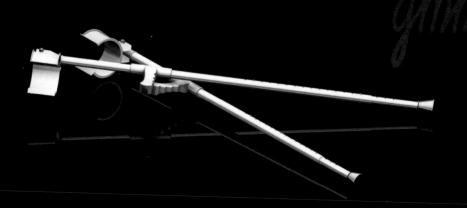

A young girl was **kidnapped** in my area 2 days before Christmas.

At first they didn't allow anyone except for the police to search for her. But after a couple days, they announced that a search party would be sent out, and anyone who wanted to help should meet at the baseball stadium.

**3,000 people** came on Christmas morning.

**GMH**

Last night, **I came home late** to find my roommate and her boyfriend cuddling on the couch. **She was sick** and couldn't sleep, and he was reading to her and **rubbing her back.**

He stayed until she finally fell asleep ... at 5 a.m.

**I found out later it was his birthday.**

**His devotion**
**GMH.**

A few years ago, my sister was diagnosed with cancer. The doctors told her that her chances of living were 1 in 1000.

Her reply? "Well then I feel sorry for the other 999 people."

She is now in remission. She GMH.

The other day, I went to the grocery store to pick up a few things.
While walking through the parking lot, I noticed a man stand on his shopping cart and give a few good pushes before *jumping on*
He smiled and laughed the entire way, *loving life.*
He was about 50 and wearing a business suit. GMH

73

when i was 15 *i tried to kill myself* by taking an entire bottle of pills. i went and laid on the top bunkbed so that i could die and then *i heard my baby brother laugh*.

*i used all my strength* to fall off my bunkbed so that someone would hear it and **find me**. i am now 29 with a college degree and newly married.

my baby brother
gives me hope

My friend Max was born deformed.
He can't use his legs at all and his hands
can only move enough to operate his chair.

He is 17.

Last weekend I saw him ride by with
A BAWLING CHILD ON HIS LAP
who had scraped her knee.

He STAYED with her and gave her
a big SMILE after she got a band-aid.

# He GMH.

When I was 4 years old, my family went on a Disney cruise. I WAS SO EXCITED... but I ended up getting seasick. ☹

As I gloomily watched the other kids play with Mickey, I felt someone tap my shoulder. IT WAS DONALD DUCK! HE STAYED BESIDE ME THE WHOLE TIME, MAKING SURE I WAS HAVING FUN.

To this day, he's still my favorite character. DONALD DUCK GMH

I was at the mall the other day when I saw an old couple sitting together. The man looked over at the woman and said,

"Jane, we did it. We grew old together."

The look in her eyes GMH.

Last year, my boyfriend lost his battle with cancer. It's been very hard since.

But this year on Valentine's Day, I received a package in the mail with a beautiful necklace and a note that said, "I wasn't ready to say goodbye just yet."

Even though his life has ended, his love has not.

His love GMH.

I work in a bank, a place where **good news** is hard to come by recently.

Today, I spoke with a gentleman who told me he needed to know how much money he had. When I asked if he had a <u>large purchase</u> coming up, he said yes. "I'm buying clothes for the <u>man who asks me for a quarter</u> every day on my way to school," he replied.

This gentleman was 12.
# GMH

I am 46 years old.

I went to the plastic surgeon for a consultation.

The doctor looked at me and said,
"Don't do this.
You're too beautiful
just the way you are.
Don't change."

That doctor gmh.

My stepmother worked at a gas station.

A blind man came in every day, and in his wallet the bills were folded into shapes.

One day he was paying for his drink and handed her a hundred dollar bill.

She immediately told him and his response was "I know. You deserve it for being honest."

His kindness GMH

81

My grandmother died today, so I took a walk to try to calm down but ended up crying on a bench. A man tapped me on the shoulder and handed me a beautiful bouquet of flowers. He said, "I saw you were crying, so I got you these," and walked away.

Strangers
GMH.

I was at a bookstore and an obscure author was doing a book signing. Nobody was coming over, he looked dejected.

Then three teenagers came over, got his autograph & took pictures with him. It looked like it made his day.

Later, I talked to them and they said they had never read his books. GMH

My little eight-year-old sister has leukemia. Today, I visited her in the hospital and she said to me:

"Ellie, I know I'm going to die. But I know that I'm going to be coming back as a kitten. So after I'm gone, when a kitten comes to your door, it will be me. Even when I'm a cat."

Her beautiful words GMH.

# I'M 22 YEARS OLD
and I'm about to go on my first date.

*I've never felt so beautiful.*

# Just today,

*I found out the real reason of my parents' death when I was 10.*

When our car lost its brakes and was going to crash into another, they tried to protect me at the last minute.

THEIR BODIES WERE FOUND, COVERING ME WHILE I WAS UNCONSCIOUS.

*Their never-ending love truly GMH.*

I use a power wheelchair on a college campus. One day, my chair battery died in the middle of campus with 3 more classes to attend and *no way to get there*.

I quickly became a **human baton**, my 300-pound wheelchair being pushed though the rain by a **series of strangers**. I got to each of my classes and back home on time!

## THANK YOU RELAY TEAM...

### YOU GMH

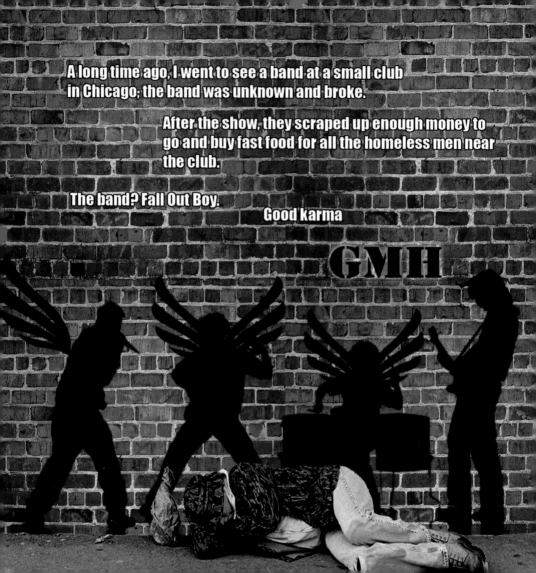

When I entered middle school I saw this super cute seventh grade boy.

I liked him ever since that day even though we NEVER talked.

Then one day in my sophomore year he came up to me during lunch.

He said, "You know, I've always thought you were beautiful."

That blew me away!

We have been married for 11 years.

TO THIS DAY HE GIVES ME HOPE

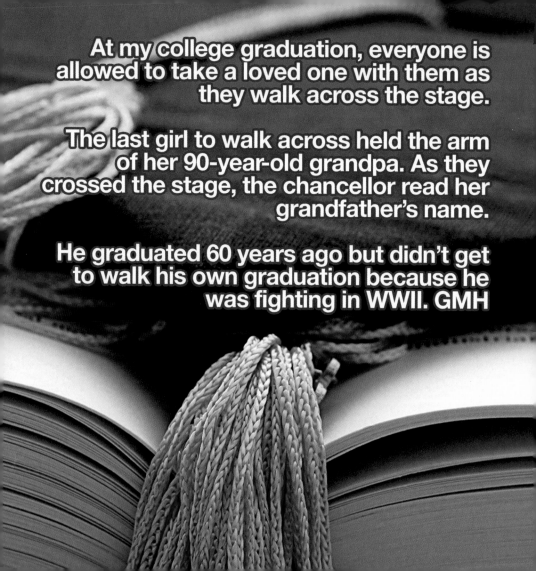

At my college graduation, everyone is allowed to take a loved one with them as they walk across the stage.

The last girl to walk across held the arm of her 90-year-old grandpa. As they crossed the stage, the chancellor read her grandfather's name.

He graduated 60 years ago but didn't get to walk his own graduation because he was fighting in WWII. GMH

I once drove a normal-looking teenager from the airport to downtown Toronto in my taxi.

For an hour we talked, and he asked me questions about my life, my family, everything.
When we arrived, he asked me what the biggest tip I'd ever received was.

I told him $80.

He gave me a $100 tip and walked off.

There's a really beautiful freshman in our school who a mentally challenged sophomore boy has a huge crush on.

SHE GOT ASKED BY AT LEAST 10 PEOPLE TO

THE WINTER FORMAL DANCE, BUT SHE DECIDED TO

GO WITH THE MENTALLY CHALLENGED BOY.

Beautiful girls who are also beautiful

inside GMH.

WHEN MY SISTER WAS YOUNGER
SHE CAME HOME FROM SCHOOL ONE DAY
AND DEMANDED I TAKE HER TO THE LIBRARY
SO SHE COULD GET BOOKS ON

# sign language.

SHE TOLD ME THERE WAS
A NEW KID AT SCHOOL WHO WAS
DEAF AND **she wanted to befriend him.**

Today, I stood beside her
at their wedding
watching her sign "I DO"

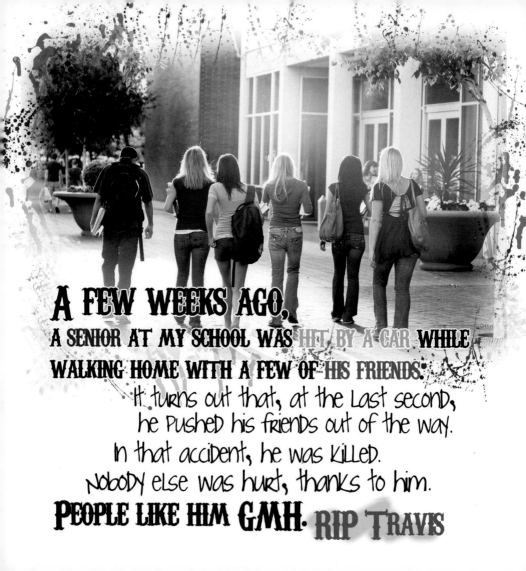

A FEW WEEKS AGO, A SENIOR AT MY SCHOOL WAS HIT BY A CAR WHILE WALKING HOME WITH A FEW OF HIS FRIENDS. It turns out that, at the last second, he pushed his friends out of the way. In that accident, he was killed. Nobody else was hurt, thanks to him. PEOPLE LIKE HIM GMH. RIP TRAVIS

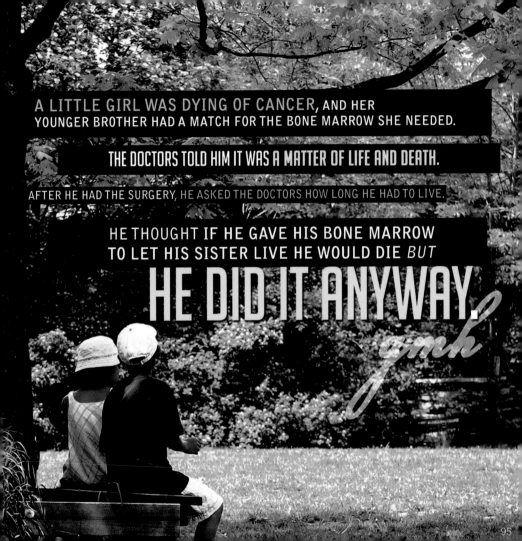

A LITTLE GIRL WAS DYING OF CANCER, AND HER
YOUNGER BROTHER HAD A MATCH FOR THE BONE MARROW SHE NEEDED.

THE DOCTORS TOLD HIM IT WAS A MATTER OF LIFE AND DEATH.

AFTER HE HAD THE SURGERY, HE ASKED THE DOCTORS HOW LONG HE HAD TO LIVE.

HE THOUGHT IF HE GAVE HIS BONE MARROW
TO LET HIS SISTER LIVE HE WOULD DIE *BUT*

# HE DID IT ANYWAY.

*gmh*

My friend and I were asked by a child if we were brother and sister.

I'm black, and my friend is white. **I said yes.**
The little kid seemed satisfied.

The future generation's acceptance **GMH.**

Today is my birthday.

A couple months ago I was attacked by a dog that left horrendous scars on my face.

My boyfriend made a book that says, "You're the most beautiful thing I have ever seen" in over 100 different languages.

97

Yesterday, my husband told me he'd be coming home in 6 days.

Today, he was killed on a mission in Iraq. He is gone at 23. I fell to the floor.

An hour later, his 17-yr-old sister was on the floor reading me the letters he sent her about his love for us.

SELFLESS TEENAGERS BIKING 4 MILES

TODAY, MY AUNT DRAGGED ME ALONG TO THE MALL TO GO SHOPPING. WHILE IN THE STORE, SHE CRITICIZED ME, CALLING ME *FAT* AND COMPARING ME TO *UGLY BETTY*.

WHEN I WALKED OUT OF THE STORE, A BOY HELD THE DOOR OPEN AND WHISPERED *"I don't know what she's talking about."*

I was reading about a little kid whose mom
told him the key to life was happiness.
When he was in school the teacher asked
them to write down what they wanted to
be when they grew up.

**He said**
**HAPPY**

They said he didn't
understand the assignment.

He said they didn't understand life.
My generation
**GMH**

A 5-year-old boy in my town had leukemia.

His wish for *Make-a-Wish* was to spend a day with Corbin Bleu (an actor in High School Musical), and he had a blast.

Yesterday was the boy's funeral. Corbin flew in to our town with his dad and attended the funeral as a pallbearer.

*His selflessness* GMH

YESTERDAY. IT WAS LATE AND I WAS HEADING TO MY CAR IN THE PARKING LOT AFTER WORK AND THREE YOUNG GUYS COME UP TO ME AND START TALKING. I WAS SCARED, UNTIL ONE DRAPED HIS ARM AROUND ME AND SILENTLY SHOWED ME A TEXT ON HIS PHONE TELLING ME THERE WAS A DODGY GUY FOLLOWING ME AND THAT THEY WOULD MAKE SURE I GOT TO MY CAR SAFELY.

THEIR KINDNESS GMH.

The other day, I was being picked on at school as usual when I felt a sticky post-it note being taped to my back.

Thinking it said "Kick Me" or something along those lines, I ripped it off and was about to throw it away when I saw that it said:

It made my day, and **GMH.**

103

I had found out that my daughter had not been going out for recess.

When I questioned her, she said she wanted to stay in and clean the hallway.

Why?

There was a new girl in her class in a wheelchair and it was tough for her to get around the halls.

Megan, I love you!

You *gmh!*

Today my 7-year-old daughter gave my 5-year-old son **A KISS ON THE CHEEK.**

After she walked away, I saw him **RUBBING THE SPOT** where she had kissed him.

I asked if he was **WIPING THE KISS OFF.**

He said, **"No, I'm RUBBING it in so it gets to my heart FASTER."**

Siblings that truly love each other

*gmh*

WHEN I WAS IN KINDERGARTEN, ONE OF MY CLASSMATES, **EMMA**, WAS DIAGNOSED WITH AML - A VERY RARE AND AGRESSIVE FORM OF **LEUKEMIA.**

SHE WAS GIVEN **4 months** TO LIVE.

EMMA TOLD OUR CLASS NOT TO WORRY, because she is stronger than cancer.

THIS YEAR SHE WILL BE WALKING THE STAGE AT HER **HIGH SCHOOL GRADUATION.**

EMMA, YOUR DETERMINATION AND STRENGTH *gmh.*

107

My uncle volunteers as a Santa every year. Today, a little girl came up and said

"I want food for my baby brother"

who was in his mother's arms nearby. When they left, a man behind them, with four kids of his own, took $100 from his wallet and insisted that she had dropped it.

Holiday spirit GMH.

If you're reading this,
I want to be the first to tell you that
YOU LOOK BEAUTIFUL TODAY.

*gmh*

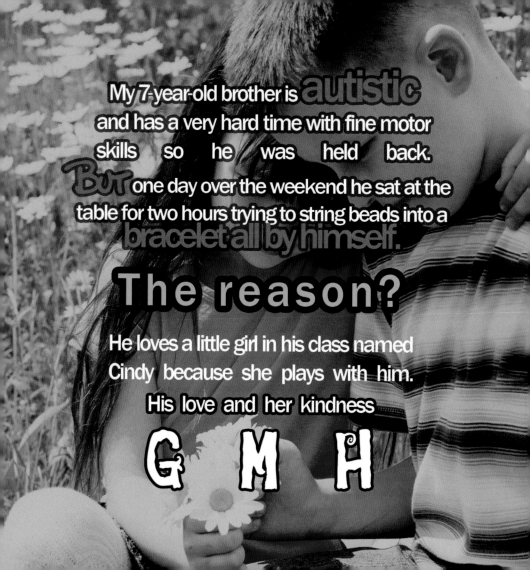

My 7-year-old brother is autistic and has a very hard time with fine motor skills so he was held back. BUT one day over the weekend he sat at the table for two hours trying to string beads into a bracelet all by himself.

The reason?

He loves a little girl in his class named Cindy because she plays with him. His love and her kindness

G M H

I WAS TALKING WITH THIS LITTLE GIRL I
USED TO BABYSIT FOR BEFORE I STARTED
COLLEGE.

I EXPLAINED TO HER THAT I'D BE GONE FOR
A WHILE AND WOULD ONLY SEE HER WHEN I
CAME HOME FOR VACATIONS.

SHE SAID, "SO YOU'LL BE GONE FOR THE
WHOLE YEAR EXCEPT SUMMER AND HOLI-
DAYS?"

I NODDED.

THEN SHE SAID, "SO YOU'RE GOING TO HOG-
WARTS?"

GMH.

YOURS SINCERELY,
DEATHROSES

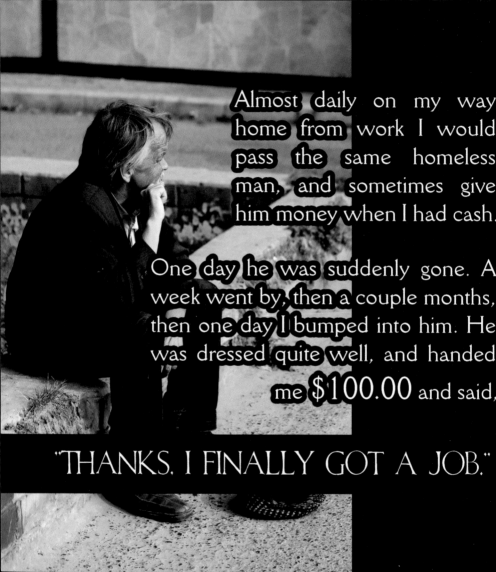

Almost daily on my way home from work I would pass the same homeless man, and sometimes give him money when I had cash.

One day he was suddenly gone. A week went by, then a couple months, then one day I bumped into him. He was dressed quite well, and handed me $100.00 and said,

"THANKS. I FINALLY GOT A JOB."

One time, I came over to my friend's house and found her and her boyfriend, sound asleep, snuggled on her couch.

The whole time he was there, she didn't brush her hair, wash her face, put on makeup, or change out of her baggy pajamas.

HE COULDN'T KEEP HIS EYES OFF OF HER

THEIR LOVE GIVES ME HOPE

I found out my cancer had returned.

I was struggling to get through the day at work without crying.
With tears in my eyes I left the classroom when my
non-verbal autistic student chased after me.

He hugged me and said:

"Smile. Don't cry!"

These were his first words.
His perseverance and love gmh.

IN JULY OF 1992, A GIRL SAT DOWN ON THE CURB OF A SIDEWALK TO TAKE A BREAK FROM A LONG RUN.

AFTER A MOMENT, she heard a NOISE FROM THE GARBAGE CAN NEXT TO HER.

HESITANT, SHE OPENED IT UP TO find a BABY, NOT EVEN A WEEK OLD, LYING INSIDE.

18 YEARS LATER, HERE I AM, FOREVER GRATEFUL TO THE beautiful angel WHO IS NOW MY SISTER.

LILLY, YOU *gmh*.

When I was six, a man came up to me and told me that he liked my glasses.

I was the only kid in my class with glasses, so I was always teased about them, but after that small comment, they didn't bother me anymore.

That man? Paul David Hewson - better known as Bono.

ROCKSTARS WHO HAVE TIME FOR LITTLE GIRLS WHEN THE PRESS ISN'T WATCHING GMH.

A long time ago, I was on the verge of committing suicide when a guy came to the roof to have lunch.

He saw me climbing over the railing and asked me to share his lunch with him.

After receiving my puzzled look, he explained,

# "EVERYONE SHOULD DIE HAPPY. OR AT LEAST WITH A FULL STOMACH."

We celebrated our **10TH WEDDING ANNIVERSARY** last month.

gmh.

At a grocery store I work at, a young lady with a baby just got done scanning her cart full of groceries but both of her cards were denied and she had no cash. She quietly asked to have them put back, when the man behind her smiled and said, "I'll pay for them."

THEY WERE TOTAL STRANGERS

One day in 5th grade, I came home upset and told my parents that my friend had been taken out of class by Child Protection Services.

My dad did everything he could to find her.

Now, for the past 11 years, I've had the sister I always wanted.

**My Parents**

**GMH**

I have a *heart defect* that's incurable resulting in *minor* heart attacks & fainting spells. One day after a nasty episode, I posted a vlog crying about how I felt helpess.

The next morning, I learned 10,000 dollars had been donated in my youtube name to the

# FIGHT AGAINST HEART DISEASE,

anonymously

*gives me hope*

*secret admirer*

THREE YEARS AGO, ALMOST TO THE DAY, I LEFT A NOTE IN A GUY FROM MY FRENCH CLASS' TEXTBOOK ASKING HIM TO **CALL me**

THAT DAY, BEING THE LAST DAY OF SCHOOL AND THE LAST DAY I WOULD EVER SEE HIM, I TOLD HIM TO CHECK INSIDE HIS BOOK, BEFORE I RAN AWAY.

*we're still together* TAKE THAT CHANCE

Today, I was in the feminine-products aisle when a middle-aged man started asking me what brand I liked to use and which were the most effective, etc.

It turns out that he is a single father to a preteen girl with Down's syndrome, and he was trying to find out which products work the best for his little girl.

Caring, loving fathers

GMH

Today, I found GSMH.

After reading all the
heartwarming stories,
I walked into my room,
and tore my suicide
journal to shreds.

I'm shaking out of happiness.

GSMH.

A BOY WAS DYING OF CANCER
and needed an expensive brain surgery,
but his family, broke and desperate, couldn't afford it.

His 8 yr old sister Tess took her piggy bank savings
to a pharmacist in order to buy a "MIRACLE."

It just so happens that the right man witnessed the
little girl's tears at the pharmacy counter: a neurosurgeon.

He performed the surgery for free.

gmh.

Today when I was working, an adorable older couple came through my line. When I asked if they had found everything they needed, the woman looked at her husband and said "I found everything I needed 43 years ago." GMH.

125

*A*N ELDERLY LADY CAME TO MY REGISTER AND WAS BUYING MILK AND BREAD.

She didn't have enough money and had no way of paying. There was a 12-year-old boy buying a video game and a toy.

**He handed me his gift card to buy her items.**
*H*E SAID SHE NEEDS FOOD MORE THAN HE NEEDS A VIDEO GAME.

*Boys like him GMH.*

**JERRY,** high school janitor, took the time to know outcasts and struggling kids. He always had candy and nice words.

One girl was struggling a lot. He made her a deal, if she graduated, he would dye his hair pink.

3 years later, she graduated. Our janitor now has pink hair. Doing more than your job GMH

127

I WAS DIAGNOSED WITH A SEVERE MENTAL DISEASE ABOUT A YEAR AGO. MY BOYFRIEND HAS PUT UP WITH ALL OF MY PARANOIA, ANGER AND ODD THINGS THAT I DO.

WHEN I TOLD HIM HE SHOULD LEAVE ME BECAUSE IT WASN'T FAIR TO HIM, HE SAID,

**"If I can't take you at your worst then I don't deserve you at your best."**

His unconditional love

GMH

I WAS WEARING A SHORT-SLEEVED SHIRT FOR THE FIRST TIME IN YEARS.

I WAS NERVOUS THAT WHEN MY BOY-FRIEND SAW MY SCARS HE WOULDN'T WANT TO BE WITH ME ANYMORE.

INSTEAD HE KISSED MY SCARS AND TOLD ME THAT IF I EVER FELT BAD ENOUGH TO HURT MYSELF AGAIN THAT HE WOULD TAKE THE PAIN INSTEAD.

HE GMH

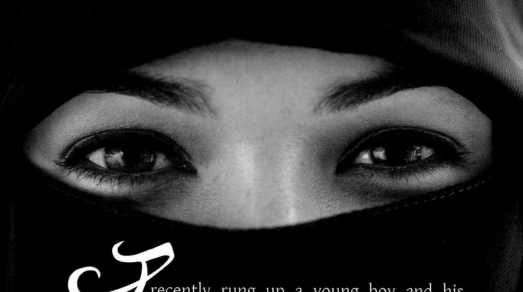

*I* recently rung up a young boy and his mother. When he saw me at the register, wearing a hijab, he grinned broadly at me. As they were walking away afterwards, he tugged on his mom's sleeve and said,

"Did you see her, ma? She's **gorgeous!** I bet that's why she's all covered up."

# He GMH

I was at the hospital yesterday.

My mum (who works in a secondary school) saw one of her students. She had been diagnosed with cancer 2 years ago.

**She's lost all her hair, has had 2 ribs taken out, part of her breast bone out, and had more operations than I can count on TWO hands.**

*Today, she was given the all clear. That girl is 15.*
**She GMH.**

My family and I disowned my sister
for her years of drug and alcohol abuse.
I found out she was in a homeless shelter so I
picked her up and took her in.
She has been sober for a year and helps my
brother every day with his baby because his
wife is terminally ill with cancer.

Now, she is the one holding the family together.

GMH

I work at McDonald's and had to work the drive-thru last night.

Even with my coat and longsleeve shirt,
I was still freezing.
A woman walked to my window and said
"Sweetie, my husband came here
earlier and said
you looked very cold."

She handed me a brand new
scarf, hat, and gloves and left.

She GMH

I've been struggling with an eating disorder for years and weigh myself obsessively throughout the day.

This morning, there was a post-it note covering the numbers on my scale that said, "You're beautiful."

I live with three guys. Men like that GMH

Before this book went to press, we asked the GivesMeHope online community to answer the question "Who gives *you* hope?" On the following pages is what they said.

· AnnieChittaphong Sengchanh · AnnieDang Our · AnnieFrank Matt · AnnieGarcia Hannah · AnnieGauhar My · AnnieGryz Ryan · AnnieHu My · AnnieLee Bonnie · AnnieManwell Randi · AnnieMilroy Julie · AnniePark Jan · AnniePham My · AnnieRhodes Anna · AnnieRoger My · AnnieTreggage Kimberly · AnnieWebb Emily · AnnieWilliams Mikelle · AnnieWilliams Taylor · AnnieYoung-Merritt Katie · AnnikaAriel Clarinet · AnnikaPrevis Krista · AnnWashenko children · AnonymousNinjaa Jerrica · AnsleyChea Savannah · AntelanaAlexandre · Jean · AnthonyEmm Cindy · AnthonyGarrett Jenna · AnthonyGrigas Sami · AnthonyKneipp Emily · AnthonyLangford Anthony · AnthonySmith Kelly · AnthonyTroiano · Abigal · AntonJo-JustOCottis · AntonioMiranda Pedro · AntonioSanturnb Jenna · AnushreeAgrawal Anshika · AnzaSyed Aari · ApA_A rvAaMuppala Srilakshmi · AprilAmao Xochitl · AprilDennen Emma · AprilEspinoza Gloria · AprilFischer Sean · AprilPedras Gloria · AprilMadduel Lucy · AprilStinson Constantine · AprilWoods Tyrone · AosaraPerera Jessica · AqsaPervaiz Neelam · ArabMetthmano Deborah · ArdenHarvey Ariel · AremBayar Imran · AriadnaGonzalez · Mother · ArianaCunha Ariana · ArianaHumphrey Diane · ArianaStone Laurie · AnanaZhang Fuli · AriannaMelian Morgan · AriannaMettinano Sarah · AriannaMersiann Miguel · ArielBradford Ursula · ArielDayan friend · ArielFontaine Dominique · ArielleHarrison Merin · ArielNelson Julia · ArielMladson Julia · ArielMartin Sophia · Andrew · ArielVeroline Mom · ArielYang Yexus · ArielYoung Laura · AriFernandez Yek · ArinaAchari Rick · ArizonaLancelevre Jonathan · AronRusci Rick · ArrayizzyPhilip Madeleine · ArthurHarry Fernanda · ArtPitchford Daniel · ArynnPalmiscano Aynne · AsayPalmiscano · AshBurnGrimm friend · AshGibby William · AshimaGupta Ravi · Tyler · Ash-LeeMontry Simon · AshitakaKleo Mark · AshliCy Vanessa · AshiaPlaisted Leo · AshleeBrown Nellie · AshleeChatten Rissa · AshleeHerberger Peter · AshleeKagome Ashlee · AshleeMartin · AshleighPullen Louise · AshleighRutzel Amy · AshleighWood Dylan · AshleighEdwards Rachel · AshleighHolder Sophia · AshleighKotula Mallory · AshleighKristy Joshua · AshleighPreston Becky · AshleyAtanasoff John · AshleyBeaton Brendan · AshleyBennett Tony · AshleyBergner Reggie · AshleyBloodgood Ashley · AshleyBolger Jon · AshleyBrooke Kaitlyn · AshleyBurton Stephanie

Marie Ryan · BronwynMurphy Ariel · BronwynWalker Sasha · BrookeAshlinPoll Cody · BrookeJahnke Amber ·
BrookeLoudon Jordan · Brooke Metzker Mary · BrookeMichelle Ranna · BrookeRhoads Caroline · BrookeSmith Kaitlyn · BrunoTexeira Jessika ·
BrookeTaylor Kimberly · BrooklynElizabeth Brook · BrooklynHuntington Bentley · BrooklynMinnie Autumn · Brook-LynnZemeer Nicole · BrooklynWalker Lyndsey · Bruno Texeira Jessika ·
Bryan&Bombard Grass · BryanaLabombard gianna · BryanChong Emily · BryanaGracia Melina · BryanMoof Rochelle · BryanMaNelson Ryan · BryonAGraland Hannah ·
Hailey · BryceHittel Hailey · BrydenGail Cissy · BrytanBorovsky David · BrytdalynnP'age Max · BryanMoof Rochelle · BryonGraham Matena · Buffy Jones Sam ·

ColleenGresk Meghan · ColleenKeeler Dreamers · ColleenKjellberg Scott · ColleenTorrey Douglas · ColleenWurtz Michael · CollinLloyd Gloria · ColtanDonaghy Ramzie · ColumbusOhio
Grace · ConnieLevitsky Gaille · ConnieMarz Steve · ConnorMartin Aubrey · ConnorSmith Allie · ConorWescox Liliana · CooperAllen David · CoralieDomenichini Myriam · CoralieWhittle
Daniel · CordeliaLang Emily · CorderoEstrada brother · CoreyKarnes Christine · CoreySuckling Sammy · CoreyWright Shayna · CorinnaFink Jesus · CorinneSnipes Eric · CorneliaMu
Grace · CorneliaBl Jesus · CornMakl Dan · CorrieBurke Jesus · CorrieBurke sister · CorrieyBernella Justine · CortneyBell Barbara · CortniBernhart David · CorwynBaesman Bryan
WendyGoweil Chris · CourtneyBaker Cassi · CourtneyBale Cassi · CourtneyCollins Donna · CourtneyCulbreath Tim · CourtneyElston Diane · CourtneyErin Nathan · CourtneyFavaloro Laura
CourtneyFriese Collin · CourtneyFulz Chyenne · CourtneyGamblin Richard · CourtneyHalley Jeffery · CourtneyHarrison Sally · CourtneyHarvey James · CourtneyIrwin Robson Zachary
CourtneyJohansson Kimberly · CourtneyJohnson David · CourtneyKlebacher Soldiers · CourtneyLawrence Sharon · CourtneyMaxwell Lindsey · CourtneyMott Kyle
CourtneyMyrden Susie · CourtneyPaige Heather · CourtneyPenzo Heather · CourtneyReeves Natalee · CourtneyRobson Zachary · CourtneySanford-Canta Ariel · CourtneySmith Riley
CricketLeague Joel · CrislynMitchell John · CrissyEspino Lexy · CristianaAmaya Edwin · CristianaManchester Sonia · CristinaMohazab Ahmad · CourtneyWilkerson Lunique · CraigBehal Tommie
CristinaMartinez Maria · CristineEstrada GMH · CristinRamolete Ryland · CristinFrederick Di · CrystaCarter mom · CrystalMays Gavin · CrystalParker Joseph · CrystalPeterson–Wantland Eric · CrystalFerrett Elizabeth
CrystalHalden Jaz · CrystalHidalgo Ryan · CrystalKayy Karla · CrystalMian Joseph · CyDenton Al · CyntaLavanja sister · CynthiaBanales
Tammy · CynthiaCaridad Stephanie · CynthiaEngle Felicia · CynthiaGuerrero · CynthiaNguyen Susan · CynthiaRobinson My · CynthiaSalmon Patrice · CynthiaWeller Sabrina
MariKrovskaya-Brahincke · OscarForrajes Felicia · DaakotaVedvik Evan · DaelShannon Liliana · DaisyPerez Emily · DakotaCarter Di · DakotaValdez Anita · DaleAdam Fraser
DallasGoulait Jamie · DallasJohnson Autumn · DallyBellafatto Dana · DaltonBrasington David · DaltonMead Joy · DamanSchreiner Brittany · DamaraHardeal Alisha · DamarraJoerg Taliyah
DamaskBrown My · DamaskTalany-Brown Barney · DamianAhmadyar Colleen · Dana Diany · DanaBui Menuda · DanaCelestino Linda · DanaDesmond Poppins · DaneNash Daria
DaneSchafzky Leanne · DaneThe Steph · DanaGordon-wallace Oprah · DanaMarie Kai · DanaMendoza Barry · DanaNanni Tony · DanaSchede Catey · DanaVespoli
Silver · DanaYovel Jesse · DanielleAtwood Jason · DanceRegnier Lisa · DaniArocha Katelynn · DaniBakalar Korrine · DaniSather Zach · DarrenLeon Laura
DarbyJoMcKie Maheen · DarbyMcKie Maheen · DarlaFremmerlid Amanda · DarlaMillian Anna · DarciAldrich Zachary · DarcIClahoun Jesus · DarciDietrich Eric · DarciePudwill Lilly · D'arcy-StarrEther Patrick
DarianAllen Michele · DanianRene A© Kim · DarlaJones Courtney · DarleneKim Leang · DarlenneMapother Belbi · DaronBrandow Mari · DarrahPeklak Zach · DarrenLeon Laura
DarrylChandler Denis · DarrylWendt Anacani · DarshiniMahendran Vivian · DarylTham Koala · DarylWinter-Pham Brad · DashaBla Paul · DashiaFortunello Lysette
DavidLawton Katie · DavidMeyer Gabriel · DaviddMcClellan Jesus · DavidPereira Victoria · DavidPhillips Tessa · DavidSaad Chelsea · DavidShelley Lyle · DavidTurley Dave · DavielMercer
Karen · DavinaFaust Mary · DavinaSmith-Perez Russell · DawnBeezley Travis · DawnMills Dylan · DayCutongco Li · DayineraVillers Taelon · DayIaWeskamp Victoria · DaynaGilmore Valorie
Henry · DaylsiFernandez Vianey · DazzWeb Rebbeca · DeandMartinez Daulton · DeannaClark Judy · DeannaFaunce Jim · DeannaGradwell Sophie · DeannaNguyen
DebbieMangereffeh Andre · DebbieMoran John · DebijanKonar Shilpi · DebbieSavvas Helen · DebraBeriton Cloyce · DeeAnnPruitt Sami · DeedeeBose Alexis · DeemaGoodbe Deema
DeannaStevens Russell · DindraaVezinaw Kevin · DeLannaGrube Nick · DelanaWilkinson Cody · DeloresHazim · DeloreyBag Erin · DelaneyGraham Maria · DelaneyPratt Kevin
Christi · DollyPorto Jo · DominicSchnabel Leslie · DominicVillaneuva Andrea · DonaldDow Stephanie · DonalPandson Stacy · DonnaPoodia Christopher · DoranC.Valentine Lilla · DorneTeri Janine
John · ElizabethRiler Denisse · ElizabethRolfe Keli · ElizabethRoss Cassie · ElizabethWarner Josh · ElizaByrne Madeleine · EliraMarshall Alec · EliraKelly Bradley · EllaCruz Irish · EllaMaster Mary
EllenMcmanus Shane · EllenVia Jayda · EdwinA.Figueroa Ann · EdwinCastillo Karla · EdwinFigueroa Ann · ElleCole Alison · ElleConnell Katie · ElleParker Huart · EllenPennetta Shaylyn

Haimann • HemicaHasan • HennaButt Wasim • HenrietteViljoen Gabrielle • HenryVasquez Jill • HiepTran Russell • HillaryCrighton Molly • HillaryAmacher Christopher • HillaryFrame Ben • HillarySchumacher Christopher • HimalFamil Family • Himashua● Anubha • HiramMinakata dad • HishamBasheer Najma • HiJAcacia Alessia • HJKwon Cheryl • Hmblik Nimu • HoldenMontgomery Ali • HolidayNewton Scott • HollandGreene Gina • HollieBentley Tom • HollieDeBaro Kimber • HollisCuffie Hollie • Holly Redfearn HollyMarieBarnett Tara • Holly Maryland Pitches Eleanor • HollyMichelleBurrell Grandma • HollyNolan George • HollyRedfearn Granda • HollyRoth Katie HollyCary HollyWatts Cary • HollyWilton Jed • HollyClode Sharon • HoneyYoung Francis • HugTruong Nathan • HonorCann Robert • HoonvashBaksi Faindeh • HopeFrench Kevin • HozelAyay Musa • HoyleWatts Gary • HuangShibei Usam • HunBa'Tai Rachel • HueiChen Yee • HugoJimenez Kimberly • HugoMuraira Giovanna • HumaHaq Shafiqa • HunterArmstrong Jonathan • HunterCharles Edo James • HuseinHussein Julie • HylanMarbach family • HugoOrtega My • IanMcDonald Brooke • IdaJensen Marthe • IlanaBajoui Sunflower • IlanaKapit Luke • ImanKarim Shonell • InolaCabatu Alexis • InaRimbu Zina • IrenaLamb Becca • IonaShepherd My • IndigoMarie Harley • IndiraSanchez Awilda • InesTan Emily • IngridMeher Mother • IraKo Sharon • IreenaNadas Zeera • IrelandArroyo Hannah • IsabelAlvarado Jacob • IsabelGrondin Talia • IsabellaBlecha Iqra Tabassum Mohammad • IrishLeh Patrick • IrskLyChorgolani Nino • InsTanael Mira • IsaacTrutwein Breeanah • IsabellaSierra Katrina • IrelandArroyo Hannah • IrmaAlexandra Jesus • InnaUrsache Peter • IrisFlower Carla • IrisLopez Mikayla • InsTanael Mira • IsaacTrutwein Breeanah • IsabellaBarker Carly • IsabellaBlecha Annemarie • IsabellaJaravata loved • IsabellaNabeelah • IsobelHutchinson Adam • IsabellMarieBrinza Anelisa • IsabellaMosqueda Heather • IsaIZepeda Jose • IshaKumar Jatin IsmailEl-Kharboitly Julie • IsmailLimbada Nabeelah • IsobelHutchinson Adam • IsabelHelfering Harrison • IsabelleTanti Saul • IsabellRobinson Joey • IsabellaShapiro Troy IvanKasapov?Casper Ham • IvelissaCruz Winnie • IvetePinkalcoas Alyssa • IvyCoop My • IvyJames Ryan • IvyOSullivan Jose • IvyPolley Loren • IvyRilea Gaga IvyGeo Biortiz • IzzyMarcuaz Oscar • IzzyDaniel Kellie • IzzyMooney Alba • IzzyZords-Garland Family • IzzyPhilip Alice • JA,rdanKim,r,A Jordan • JacalynAnn My Sarah • JackieShiffler Robert • JackieBrokaw Winifson • JackieBodsley • JacksWest Sydney • JaciaClouter Olivia • JacindaGraham Kathy • JackJazzRaul Dean • jackD0cBo0rD?' Ryan • JackieMoloney Mary • JackieNgo Wesley • JackieBurrell Tyler • JackieParker Tyler • JackieSlaughter Lisa • JackieStark Tessel Elsie • JackieRamirez Elizabeth • JackieMartinez Jacklyn Ratcliff Tyler • JackMatulich Jack • JackRaymusPecri Shannon • JackScott Tristan • JackManning my • JackMoody grandma JackyChen Suzanne • JadynAuste you • JaclynHanratty Crystal • JaclynLaSpata Katie • JaclynMa Thierry • JacobBaughman Trent • JacodChannedGreer Brittney • JacobFortner Bunny JacobGreer Brittney • JacobStevens Courtney • JacodVincent Amshan • JacquelineKan Madeline • JacquelineRose My • JacquelineWeiland Clara • JacquelineWilson Gloria • JacqueSchoeg Tim • JacquiFacaris Linda • Jada-MareeWade Kelsey • JadaSierra Katrina • JadeAnsell Shane • JadeHardy Erica • Jadei′ ej, Bonamee JaelLi honest • JadeMcDaniel Morgan • JadeMuckleston Sue • JadeWesley James • JadeYoung Rachael • JaeLee Victoria • JaelynFladger Danta • JaimayaCarter Kasey • JaideRaine Colby • Jaime-LieGillis Zoe • JaimSemenas Alex • JaimieChan Anthony • JaimiePomares Anjelica • JaimMarkeSegal Will • JaimiGerard Mazy • JakeBrion Goober • JakeHuntley Amanda JakeJohnson Jake • JakeRasch Anastasia • JakeWoodward Howard • JakkiCushing Amy • JakkyGeda jakky • JakkiBooyah Chance • JakeBrokaw Will • JudyJ JameeRooplal Zara • JamesNyugen Mason • JameyAbergo Dylan • JamesPefes Sianne • JamesHo Dakota • JamesLarson Sharon • JamesMassey girlfriend • JamesMcTaggart JamieFortier Daniel • JamieGoodermote Kaylah • JamieGuerry Bob • JamieJorgy Emma • JamieOkino Yvonne • JamieSutherd Perkins • JaninELorenzo Angela • JamieVaughan Shaun • JamieWillett JamiePark Alex • JamiePinedo Jessica • JamieRappaport Deb • JamieSchabdach beu • JamieThierry • JamieMcGhee Emily • JamieMoody grandma Charlene • JamieSnively Joel • JanAbad Araceli • JanaMatsosho Kathi • JananiKnollman Kathi • JamieTomatsky Jamie • JamieVertz Tania • JamieWillett Joseph • JanieeWilson Matt • JanelleGomez Carl • JanelleMalillano Jane • JanelleSlater Brianne • JanePark Brian • JaneTheo Steven • JanicLewke Jarod • JaniceClaris Janice Turberville Tammy • JanieKleiner Katie • JanieMcManamon Andy • JanieOkino Yvonne • JanieSutherd Perkins • JaninELorenzo Angela • JamieVaughan Shaun • JaminSingh Celina JanineSmith Nick • JaninaAnandamohan Mari • JanjiGaliLAt Luna • JanmarieePetramala Paula • JanneyPrieto-Gomez Gabriela • JapaSandhu Tejbir • JaquelyBiebel Cameron • JaquieSaysovar Zara • JamesNguen Mason • JaredManning Vale • JarredSlater Brianne • JarrodGilbert Cecilia • JarrodCinl Charlotte • JasmineCatherine • JasmineMckenney Keoni • JasmineMirajkar JaQule • JaredSipple Emily • JaredDil Anders • JasmineCrowley Shae • JasmineDevone Trent • JasmineFinnie Carl • JasmineKy Ethan • JasmineLivingston Claire • JasonOmston Anna • JasonOrtiz Mickey • JasmineBell Alexander • JasmineGrace My • JasmineKelly Ashworth Jade • JadeKellyAshworth Jade • JayGee Green • JaylaRawls Brenda • Jay-MeeSchulte-Radke Angel • JaymeHui Anita Dani • JasmineSchneider Rand • JasminWills Anne • JasonEverAert My • JasonMcintosh Caitlin • JasonFashamil Fay • JasminGuesmi Souhayl • JasmineBartley Jessica • JasonWhitmore Barbara • JasonYu Roger • JasmicRbls Jay • JaydeAfroasth Jay • JaymiAManuela • JaysonAstor Julianna • JayWeimer Andrew • JayVu Erika • JazlyneCrawley Luzard • JazmanJacob • JaydenSprague Tayla • JayKari Kual • JatnoGarcia Ana • JazmineCHild Gilliard • JazmineVaughan Michael • JazminStith Terri • JazTalbot James • JazzApont Arya • JayCherry Grace • JaydeAshworth Jade • JaylieAnisa Jenn • JaydeRondelle Rand • JasminGK Anne • JennaGk Anne • JeannieChoi Aung • JeanieKeating Aris JJBPayne Craig • JdShields Jennifer • JeannetteTsia Richard • JeannieRoque Sean • JeanieKamonWilliams Paula • JeanneKeating Aris JeannieStanley Jean • JeanNorman joshii • JeanThorson Jenny • JeffKoynychuk Beau • JeffWaggoner Kaitlyn • JeffyJordan Rosely • JehanKhanKarimMiah Mujibur JeimiMeison Gemma • JeksaDawnDoyle Karli • JeksaDoyle Karl • JelaiePeacock My • JemimahBrady Anna • JeriGray Anna • JenCart Becky • JeniferBorel Catherine Ndebonso • JeremotnTanRayHan Kimberly • JeremyWang Talia • JennyWigin Margaret • JennyGo Katherine • JenPanziarl Jerry Sam • JennyAllred Jesus • JennyBriant Freedom Sophie • JennaDawson Jennifer • JennaDickinson Taylor • JennaNagle chris • JennaOldham Scott • JennaBenningfield Danielle • JennaShearer • JennaSingh Celina Janet • JennaThompson Gayla • JennersDeCurzio person • JenNguyen Jimmy • JenniferBratton Jennifer • JenniferGuzman Acts • JenniferHarding Jane • JenniferHoang Madison • JennersBelltower Barbara • JennaLebowitz Fay • JennifferCai Clement • JennifferCampbell Kleinov • JenniferChow Rob • JenniferDegenhardt Anna • JenniferDenson Susan Wilhe • JenniferBratton Jennifer • JenniferGreenburg Allee • JenniferHopeDaniels Danny • JenniferHaskell Justin • JenniferHernandez Jennifer • JenniferHoang Megan • JessicaFralix Lisa • JessicaFord Lina • JessicaFusel Melinda • JessicaGilliard Jillian • JessicaHack Kayla • JessicaHubbert Nevin • JessicaJohnson Evan Anthony • JenniferWhipple McKenzie • JennHowley Traci • JennTheu Jenny • JennyAllred Jesus • JennyBergmann Snickels • JennyDanielChris Shella • JennySpence Jesus • JenniferSize My JennyTran Michelle • JennyWang Talia • JennyWigin Margaret • JennyGo Katherine • JenPanziarl Jerry • JennyDubose Parents • JennyMaillet Jorge • JennyAlaimo Cody Elizabeth • JessiRichmond Philip • JessicaRosenbluth Steve • JessicaRudolph Tammie • JessicaTowns Cody • JessicaLiesl Scott • JessicaSanchez Dane • JessicaRains Mary • JessicaRausch Sean • JessicaSwope FCCLA • JessicaTan My • JessicaSewart Scott • JessicaSimonson Amanda • JessicaTowns Cody • JessicaSchroeder Joanne • JessieVera Janice • JessiHartig JessicaWillhite Kelsi • JessicaWixom Amanda • JessicaWyer Justin • JessicaZamorano Ryan • JessicaPeters Jordan • JessicaSawyer Madison • JessicaBlankenship My • JessiHufschmid Nick • JessikaBumgarner Jason • JessikaKillian Tamara • JessKing Jordan • JessicaZoey Vix • JihndNugroho Bonnar • Jihae Choi Hana • Ji-HwanGuzman Guadalupe • JilLEvans Emma • JillHazlitt Pitts Cody • JilinZhang Kaitlyn Lucas • JessieGray Bramstead • JessieMartinez Julian • JessikaLoading Emily • JessieNat Carly • JillMcNamara-Twiss Eric • JillPorciuncula Dennis • JillRoss daughter • JilSchwarz Adam • JimAmbrose family Breanne • JessyJennings Family • JessyWalters Gavin • JessZetts Doug • JessZeidas Gina • JeuYuki • Jewellahoward Alisa • JhazziPitts Cody • JillianFitzgerald Ryla • JillianGorman Sean • JessicaNoelWehby Heidi • JessicaNorthrop Josh • JessicaO′Loughlin Judy • JessicaMilling Cody • JhenaldySullivan Joe • JessicaPercy Random • JessicaFlanery Savio • JoannaGarratt Jane • JoannaSchuckert My • Jessi-JayFatty ideat Jerlene • JieZhou Vix • Jihindnugroho Bonnar • JiJIKyn My • JJerardo Yuki • JiMatalam Enzo • JoanPaez Ryan • JoannaFoong boyfriend • JoanGott Christopher • JillianGorman Colin • JessicaSoler Joshua • JessikaSanford Dennis • JitskaymeClar Albert • JioBonatti Noah • JessikaAire Noah • JonnChristopher Jasmine • JoanPowell Christopher • JoanneReid Paul • JoAnnResner Dustin • JoBurdett Gina • JoannaTrinidad Francis • JillSoler Joshua • JiselleHall mum • JiJiKonnieLove Whitney • JoAnnChristopher Jasmine • JoAnneAire Noah • JoAnnResner Dustin • JoAnnPowell Christopher • JoanneReid Paul • JoBurdett

Josh · KaylaTolkov Christine · KaylaTran Amy · KaylaTrojani Jenny · KaylaZabala God · KaylaZayas Jeanette · KayleeAnna Shelby · KayleeBliss
Cody · KayleeBrow Jordan · KayleeClifton Dedication · KayleeDanielle Kathryn · KayleeGinord Lilly · KayleeHerda Jessica · KayleeSwabb Samantha · KayleeWalker
Alana · KayleighDagsher Chris · KayleighDobson Ellie · Kay-LeighGavin Taylor · Kayleighlynn thompson · KaylinLarkin Bill · KaylinPysher Becky · KaylinSchwiesow Phyllis · KaysaaLewis Maddox · KeelaTracy
Blair · KayTierney Donna · KaytlinMaguire Ninja · KayteSaunus Carmelle · KorisRamos Paul · KeashaClairmont Jazlyne · KeeganDay Jordan · KeelaTracy
Linda · KeiraFristad Amy · KeebeeWidener Jeremy · KeriJohnson Kayci · KeriLynn Wilkey Alyssa · KeiaraNance Kelly · KeiraDychowski Friend · KeiraFiresterine Brittney · KeiraFiresterine
Kaliluh Alexandria · KellenWeigand Eliza · KelleyGunnell Bill · KelliBorden Patricia · KellieAbbott Rita · KellieBenson Travis · KellieColontrelle Matt · KellieJackson John ·
KellieLurker Brady · KellieLynJackson John · KellieMcLeod Josh · KellieMoran Riley · KellieWidener Bria · KellyBirns Kelton · KellyCullen Michelle · Kellye-Sé-S'llona · KellyFerreira Lee
KellyGondek Chris · KellyGrove Justin · KellyGuo Tysen · KellyHardin Gage · KellyHong Chong · KellyHug Bill · KellyKyms Kelton · KellyMonica · KellyPater Nic · KellySeran Chloe
Hannah · KellyTattersall-Moore Danni · KellyWilliams Leslie · KelseaBowin Friends · KelseaMcVey Vincent · KelseyAllman Kevin · KelseyBlankenship KAYLOR
Davidson · KellyMagana Robert · KellyMcLeod Josh · KelseyFlower Amelia · KelseyForqueran Stephen · KelseyHicks Alan · KelseyHull Dolores · KelseyKottle Kenya
KelseyLake Ashton · KelseyLaVare Kelsey · KelseyLou Amy · KelseyMarquith leeanna · KelseyMcCracken James · KelseyMichelleWeigand Nicole · KelseyPhipps Earl · KelseyPugh Madison
Travis · KelseeBugay Elaine · KelseeJeffrey Shelley · KelseePerry Reese · KelsieSavage Hugo · KendallLynnMikrut Kara · KendallFace Krystal · KendallSchmasha Anna
KendallWashington Nate · KendallWrite Josh · KendraBlackDaniher friends · KendraBogert Jonathan · KendraCalvan Caroline · KenellTingling Debrene
KenzieMandrake Colleen · KenzieMagee Colleen · KerilLedford Scott · KerriDanielle Cecil · KenzieRadke Cecil · KenzieRadke Cecil
KenzyForman Courtney · KerianneMagee Colleen · KeriLedford Scott · KenriDanielle Cecil · KenzieRadke Cecil · KenzieRadke Cecil
Kersch · KerseyTadeo Kysha · KristinJokfelmeier Jessica · KerstinVossberg Connor · KettieDesvallons Tonique · KettinJetShuttel Jon · KevanDunlap Kevin · KevinBrady Yashika
Alyssa · KevinFavis Patricia · KevinHipkin Emilie · KevinMills Elizabeth · KevinMurray Abraham · KevinSeeram Idemudia · KevinWinkler Alyssa · KeyaAllkira Jacob
Tyler · KieraBuckley Kyra · KieraLiontonio Joseph · KieranAshton-Jones Marjory · KieranCaldwell Daniella · KieranFitch Holly · KieranGarvey Karan · KieranWilton John · KierstenBrown Eric
Khalilames Danuali · KhernEspaExda Ian · KikiLauland Dillon · KhristianBurse Heather · KhrystaGuzman My · Kiali-RaeEmerson Denise · KiaraLyonis Kelly · KiaraNixon MJ · KiarraCraft
Mark · KimberlyBlood Theresa · KimberlyConnors Natasha · KimberlyEisner Ann · KimberlyGlambert Rachel · KimberlyHeu Kikuj · KimberlyHinz Aletha · KimberlyLam Hannah · KimberlySeed Laura
Ryan · KimberlyLionel Allison · KimberlyOakes Joey · KimberlyPellegrini Kimberly · KimberlyPrivett Jonathon · KimberlyRebarda Geeta · KimberlySeed Laura · KimberlyWatt Josephine
KimberlyStone Brett · KimLao buddy · KimMaen Robert · KimMarah Nate · KimBrabham Russell · KimCode David · KimForbes friends · KimHunterShaltuto Maia · KimikoHinx Julie
KimShina Lyndsey · KimverlyGarcia Mervin · KimNaber Patrick · KimWood Patrick · KimWivin Jeremy · KimMittgrayson Kenny · KinseyBaltzell Gale · KiraChristmas · KiranDeath Yashika
KirstinBurgard Justin · KirstinElodieSummerlin Emily · KirstinStewart Hillary · Kirsty-leeHorley Mary · KirtinQuake Cody · KourtneyDease · Cody · KourtneyRobertson Angie · KrazzyKashat Pat · KreetinCalvin My
KreitonCaldwell Naszira · KretelKh Kretel · KrisAurand Brian · Kris-HamptonBret · KrisNigel Jan · KrisRoberts Diane · KrissBlank KayLee · KrissMichael
Shane · KrissyTuazon Heman · KristaBoring Farl'a · KristenArn Matthew · KristenBryan Karan · KristenFlood Dixie · KristenGeorge Marissa · KrisStonde Beatriz · KristanRuiz Eric
Zachary · KristenLaine Renee · KristenLizer Kristen · KristenMolinaro Nancy · KristenMoreno Janice · KristenNicholePatterson Dave · KristenPage Nixon · KristenPenson Kitty
Arneen · KristenPenfield Jessica · KristenReneeivy Daniella · KristenRice God · KristenRichard Destiny · KristenStockdale Kristen · KristenWhite Bailey · KristianGonzales Emmanuel
KristianKunShina Errol · KristenAllan Amy · KristineMilfar Everyone · KristinaMuszynski Yuliya · KristinaPinjusic Kristine · KristinaVa Vincent · KristinaVillaluna Tobias · KristinHussell Charlotte
KristinKlein Nathanael · KristinLaDia Darlan · KristinaBjern Robert · KrissyMidnight Adam · Kristin-Marah Nate · Kristina Vincent · KristinaVillaluna Tobias · KristinHussell Charlotte
LauraAquino Myra · KristyGarry My · KristyMartin Victor · KystalTaylor Dakota · KristoferFreedman Luke · KristopherKurre Bernie · KristyaJuneThill SarahPeterson
KrystalJarvis Megan · KrystalShanahan Austin · KystalTaylor Dakota · KrystalValerin Ariel · KrystalVelez West Ben · Laura Johnson · LauraLeonard Marina · LauraLynn Steven · LauraMamalick
Larry · LauraMei Amil · LauraNguyen Andrea · LauraPacker Kevin · LauraParsons My · LauraRose Chloe · LauraSabrina Stephanie · LauraTimling Erika · LauraTrenholm Jansen April
LauraSilva Jeremiah · LauraSollom Sean · LauraStargel Natalie · LauraStreeter My · LauraTimling Erika · LauraTrenholm Jansen April
Christina · LaurenFinch Jennie · LaurenLeiman Anna · LaurenLewis Kristy · KyleMcClawTammy · KyleMcCormick Kay · LaurenMartin Natalia · LaureMcKinney Robert · LaurenNeal Elizabeth
aunt · LaurenAyala Kevin · LaurenBachle Jennifer · LaurenBaggott Tom · LaurenBlackwell Amanda · LaurenChurchman Mother · LaurenClemm God · LaurenComp
Kelly · LaurenCramer Cass · LaurenDencePedreck Jacob · LaikynPavey Keri · LaaceyMurray Courtney · LaceyParks Matt · LaceyStaples Christian · LaceyTedder Stewart · LachlanWall Courtney
Lucy · LaurenHill Ray · LaurenHooper Everyone · LaurenHughes larissa · LaurenHunt Betty · LaurenHunterRogers Paul · LaurenIngram Seth · LaurenJohnson Mother · LaurenJordan Amy
Meghan · LaurenMichael Jacob · LaurenMiranda Conner · LaurenMorley BreeEppelstun · LaurenNogay Cathy · LaurenPaige Bailey · LaurenPenzien Jon · LaurenPinto Matthew
Carrie · LaurenStockton Jess · LaurenTurfrey Gareth · LauriArnold Callum · LaurieBeardsworth Cassie · LaurenStirton Barbara
Dianna · LazzmoMervin Doral · LeahAdam buddy · LeahMavin Robbins · LeahStevens Austin · LeahWaldoniged Reafan · LeanWelch God · LeahEvy
Nicholas · LeahRavniak Daniel · LeahSimmons Jesus · LeahHenke Donna · LeahNorma God · LeahMcDonald Dillon · LeaJordaderdan Helene
Brenna · Lendyl Lyman Matthew · LennoxMcGooseo Kristen · LennyPaulo April · LeoKelly Vivienne · LesleyRamirez Daniel · LesleyRead Dezaun · LeslieBoud Rebecca
LeslieOlion Mark · LeslieRaezer Austin · LeslyRitz Ernesto · LettieYoung Jean · LexiWright Jean · LexiGibson Jennifer · LeysenHo
Ashley · LexMarbles Yasmin · LiamStewart Kaleb · LiamCrowe Liam · LiamElira Linai · LiamWare Elma · LianaRose Serena · LianneKoote Eoin · LibbyAnderson Adam · LibbyCarrico
Kelsy · LieBastos Yasmin · LiahSherwat Ralph · LibbyThorkildsen Ella · LibbyLayne Josh · LiddyJordan Christy · LieKok Hillary · LieKlein Shira · LeeseyRavHollsander Haley · LiesAFawcett Bobby
Steven · LiesenHolt Hilary · LilaShrat Shamalee · LiivASJamus Trimu · LiliacBlack Jake · LilianGaddi Noni · LilianNguyen Lilian · LilaScholt Family · LiliaTillman Cowell · LilianFaran Stephanie
Donna · LilyBuchholz Tom · LillRithe Alfredo · LilWenstein Zachary · LilliumSamuel · LinK.. Ey Alisson · LinaBrevik K · LindaFekonja Haris · LindaBernard-Crowe My · LindaMichelle Andy
LindaPAGrukel Dianne · LindaXiao Family · LindsayIversen Derek · LindsayLovold Heather · LindsayNaumann Allie · LindsayShaeWoodcock Ripley · LindsayStocks Mimi · LindsayToothaker

Sarah • OliviaJucha enrique • OliviaLanger Adam • OliviaLeighByers Sarah • OliviaMcDaniel Ben • OliviaMcKay Catherine • OliviaMonast steven • OliviaNiedzialek Anna • OliviaParziale Lonnie • OliviaPastures Luke • OliviaPerkins Tesslyn • OliviaSchwab Olivia • OliviaSmith Lisa • OliviaThiessen Petra • OliviaWoods Lisa • OmarElYajouri Halaz • OmarYajouri Halaz • OnyxiaGonzalez Victor • OpheliaKong Mona • OskarEdgren Katie • PaavanBuddhdev God • PabloEnamorado Connie • PacificObadiah Kelley • PaigeBarnett SB • PaigeBartholomew Leigha • PaigeEdsonn Logan • PaigeEverman Joey • PaigeHart Robin • PaigeIturbide Drew • PaigeJurgelewicz Rachel • PaigeKrupa Margaret • PaigeLett Elizabeth • PaigeMiner Morgan • PaigeNewton Hannah • PaigeNowag Dara • PaigePinney Liz • PaigePrevost Mawmaw • PaigeShaw David • PaigeSherman Jessica • PaigeVanderJagt John • PaigeVosmik Alex • PaigeWachter Samantha • PaigeWells Tyler • PaigeWilliams Charlotte • PaigeYoung Jeremy • PaisleyHarper Ian • PamelaN Sheila • PamelaPiÃ±ol Gonzalo • PamelaRodriguez Sam • PamelaSroka Daniel • PamRose Dogs • PaolaEsquijarosa Cali • PaolaGonzalez Isabella • PaolaIrary Rossy • PaolaMejia Peter • PaolaPanana Jessica • PaoloEstrella Jasmine • ParisDow Jennifer • ParkerLenamon Jonathan • PascaleErgas Patricia • PathanKhan Schol • PatriciaCo God • PatriciaCounts Tyler • PatriciaDrovdlic Patricia • PatriciaGallegos Marriam • PatriciaGlassman Theresa • PatriciaHurtado Jordon • PatriciaLy My • PatriciaMcCormack Melissa • PatriciaSarroca Melanie • PatriciaStarzxuupHurtado Jordon • PatriciaWong Helen • PatrickShutt Jessica • PattyellaHawthorne Brianna • PattyHavel Andrew • PaulbaÃ±ez Mario • Paula-Kun Madeline • PaulaMillares sisters • PaulBassinson Barack • PaulDavies Nadia • PauleeneVecino Lita • PaulGardsonLesondra Krizel • PaulinaLlano Marco • PaulineGalang Yagna • PaulinePurugganan Vic • PaulMoskowitz David • PauloSeabra sindy • PaulSteis My • PaulTruong Malika • PaulV. asia • PaxtonKrishna David • PayneSillavan Megan • PaytonGuenhwyvar Bob • PaytonMarshall Michael • PearlDar Torsten • PearlyAlarcon Lucia • PeekoDelvardes My • PeightonRay Tasha • PeninaHarrison Rivkah • PeterBeug Shannon • PeterMacfarlane Zoey • PeterShuba Nicole • PeterTrinhh Pee • PeterWoodward-Court Jessica • PetraZarbock Kitty • PetterHolstad Rebekka • PeytonAlexisChaney Paul • PeytonLangdon-Laberge David • PhilCummins Kyle • PhilipEscobedo Adam • PhilipLau Sabby • PhilipMacapaggal My • PhillipDaniels bidwell • PhillipFry Sarah • PhillTaylor God • Phoebe-ChristineMunoz Seth • PhoebeKitscha Dave • PhoebeMontgomery Jacob • PhoebePunia JP • PhoebeWightwick Izzie • PiaPoÃ¾ek NataÅ¡a. • PicklesNichols Jasmine • PilialohaGardner Ian • PiliValdes Bernardo • PiperBold Ian • PiperBold Ian • PiperKennedy Kurt • PiperLambert Ginny • PiperMatlock Tatum • PippaSouthern Em • PolinaMcGuire Andrew • PollyRawcliffe Jonny • PolyyGivesmehope Melanie • PoojaNaidu Tieman • Pooja'Pucca'Shori Maine • PoojaShori John • PoojaSuresh Prema • PoppyJones Javen • PrabhjotKaur brother • PradeepChandra Tony • PrakashKong Amanda • Pranav Menon • PrasathGomez Pepe • PratikPatel Vasu • PravaliKothakota Justin • PrestonGodkin Cloe • PrincessGoldsmith Devon • PrincessMarie Amanda • PrinceVisual-Kei Carlie • PriscillaTai Jesus • PriyaChidambaram Deivanai • PriyaDharampuriya Andrew • PriyankaPod Arjun • PriyaPuriya Rachel • PsyGiroux Barbara • PtSalirathavibhaga greg • PuneetHeer My • PutriSenja Parents • QianhuiLim Blake • QianhuiLim My • QituwraAnderson Nashiydah • QuennayPrice Clara • QuincyNg Jesus • RaashSal Tanya • RabeccaHicks Mary • RabiyaMansoor Rabiya • RachaelBevill Casey • RachaelBurton Charlie • RachaelHorwood Samuel • RachaelKnick Patricia • RachaelMarie ronda • RachaelNarbey Elizabeth • RachaelPaige Austin • RachaelPearl God • RachaelRen My • RachaelRosenberg bestfriend • RachaelSeiden Alex • RachaelValbert Nicholas • RachaelWinden Jen • RachealPaul Chris • RachelBantados Ashley • RachelBarenberg Brittany • RachelBarry Alex • RachelBeauregard Matthew • RachelBenecke Poppop • RachelBerry Virginia • RachelBlahblahblah Rachel • RachelBloom Eileen • RachelBondy Josie • RachelBrier Sarah • RachelCallari Micah • RachelCamera Rachel • RachelChan Bun • RachelChesney Kayde • RachelClark Rosella • RachelCobb anaclare • RachelCole Rachel • RachelConrad Clarissa • RachelCopans Jon • RachelCoughlin Saber • RachelCraig Wesley • RachelDaugherty J'Non • RachelDavis Nikki • RachelDennis Marilyn • RachelDutton Emma • RachelFairfield Lydia • RachelFlores Kentrell • RachelGagaAntebellum Trish • RachelGallegos Lauren • RachelHaas Logan • RachelHafer Alana • RachelHannah Alaysa • RachelHao Jotik • RachelHarris Nick • RachelHeigert Lindsay • RachelHelmandollar Cindy • RachelHettrick Orion • RachelHill Ben • RachelHumphrys Susan • Rachel-iBurlew Gallo • RachelJay Emily • RachelJohnson Adele • RachelKaneshiki Miriah • RachelKitchCole Rachel • Rachel-Landon Bryan • RachelLeigh Ian • RachelleMarcum Gail • RachellePierner-Lytge Yasher • RachelLogan Rachel • RachelLui Samuel • RachelLundberg Lisa • RachelLynn Cole • RachelMacDonald Ian • RachelMacellaro Rhiannon • RachelMain My • RachelMariePomeroy Jesus • RachelMarleyClark Rosella • RachelMaycock Kevin • RachelMcNaughton Steven • RachelMead God • RachelMikita Lauren • RachelMincey Mack • RachelMooney marty • RachelMusser Carol • RachelNguyen Chad • RachelNheu Kaye • RachelPeng Eva • RachelPham Mark • RachelPhelps Becky • RachelPomeroy Jesus • RachelPoole Chris • RachelPoshusta Max • RachelRebecca Rachel • RachelRichter Jessica • RachelRoush Megan • Rachel-RuthieLandon Bryan • RachelSczurek Elaine • RachelShaffer Joshua • RachelShelton lauren • RachelSneddon Charlie • RachelStone Edward • RachelTanner Trey • RachelThomas Friends • RachelTurnbloom Adam • RachelWalker Group • RachelWaller Christian • RachelWard Chastane • RachelWarner Patrick • RachelWhite Carol • RachelWood Ellen • RachelYanna Samantha • Rachel'Zombiie'Atkin Jessica • RachelZwick Julie • RachelZwingli Austin • Rachel?MacDonald Ian • RachÑ"IBarkÑ"rwalterstolbert Catherine • Rachyl Duffy • RacquelJoseph Dollie • RadhikaSagar Ali • RaeanneGonzales Julia • RaeEwing Kristie • RaeLopez Apolinar • RaelynDuening Elizabeth • RaeMinor Vernelle • RaeQuigley Renee • RaeVanta Shaira • RagenRoss Morgan • RaiChun My • RainaNewman Ryan • RaineDrosdick Audrey • RainSouth Luke • RaissaEsguerra Andrea • RajanDhingra Mish • RaleighChristian Tyler • RalphanthonyShinn Kara • RamanaWignarajah Vamana • RamaSabanekh Annamari • RamneekPurewal Mandeep • RamondelaRosa Antonio • Ramonla Antonio • RamseyCole Jennifer • RandaKriss Krista • RandiCarrabotta Bouncy • RandiKerr Brandon • RandiStroz Adam • RandyDeLack Amanda • RandyLivingstone dad • RandyRoy Gera • RaniaHegazy Abla • RaniSimpson Shelby • RaquelAntunes Patricia • RaquelÃYowings Robert • RaquelFernandez Graciela • RaquelMercado Savannah • RaquelVidaurri My • RavahShareef Anew • RavenFlowers Patrick • RavneetBajwa Kiran • RawanAl-Nasiri Allah • RayaBasiliali Angie • RayAtchison • RayeT Forrest • RaymelQuiÃ±ones Bethany • RaymondLin Cassandra • RazanKhan Ishwer • RcCola Weezy • ReaganPaz Taylor • ReaghanHuff Brenda • ReanneAnad River • ReanneStrauss Pehlke • Rebecca Weisselberg • RebeccaAlarcon Jamie • RebeccaAttard Agnes • RebeccaBennett Melanie • RebeccaBlankenship Julie • RebeccaBrooks Hunter • RebeccaBunn Kyle • RebeccaDougherty Peggy • RebeccaDy Barney • RebeccaEpley God • RebeccaFaust Steven • RebeccaFox Rachel • RebeccaGao Crystal • RebeccaGibbs Paul • RebeccaGoor mark • RebeccaGraham Katy • RebeccaGurwah Savande • RebeccaHasler Matt • RebeccaHebberd Bryce • RebeccaLandry James • RebeccaLaube Renel • RebeccaLeigh Cherry • RebeccaMattox All • RebeccaMoore Elaina • RebeccaNicoleSakovich Alexander • RebeccaNoel T.R. • RebeccaRandall Alistair • Rebecca-Ricochet Lawlz • RebeccaRider Rebecca • RebeccaRinke Richie • RebeccaRuhlman Family • RebeccaSakovich Alexander • RebeccaSanhueza Peter • RebeccaSimpson Marlene • RebeccaStriggow Kimberly • RebeccaWas-Here Junias • RebeccaWooten Sean • RebeccaWroe Familgy • RebecKaFrailer Gabe • RebekahAnderson Wendy • RebekahBurns Elsie • RebekahEs Thomas • RebekahJaydenClee Rebekah • RebekahLaursen Diane • RebekahLee Karen • RebekahLouisee Vanna • RebekahOrding Lee • RebekahSmith Andrew • RebekaPatrushev Deanna • RedaAbedi Allah • ReemaaSiingh Kiran • ReganMckenzie Krystal • ReganMontoya Edward • ReggieAtazar Ronald • ReginaBattista Morgan • Regina Deleonguerrero • ReginaEkaputri Shinta • ReginaMrls Irene • ReillyBriggs Illy • ReillyPeterman Roxane • RenataFriesendorff Jade • RenaWu Li • ReneAlvarenga Starr • ReneeDiaz Alexander • ReneeGluck Larry • ReneePaul Jonathan • ReneePetrosyan Christian • RenisaMaki Scott • RentonWong Amy • RenzLane Chanel • RenzoJuan Claire • ResaDean dad • RevynBrown Jesus • RewaHill Caleb • ReyneHale Shannan • RheaCarpio-Salise Boyet • RhiannaCockrell My • RhiannaRose Justin • RhianneWilliamson Renee • RhiannonEvans Lara • RhiannonGregoire Rhiannon • RhiannonThomas Sue • RhiannonYencha Libby • RhiaSteele husband • RhondaHawkins Cory • RianaRevis My • RiannonMoreno Shayne • RiaSharma kate • RibynHall Mom • RicaraMcDrago Jack • RichardAkamine Kacie • RichardBargielski Tammy • RichardDuong Rachel • RichardPartridge Kaitlyn • RichieCornell Marissa • RickCarpenter Shawnee • RickeyShotwell Sara • RickHernandez Ali • RickTurk Carla • RickyAvila Madeline • RickyHallstead Marbear • RiczTomas Charmaine • RikaShinsato God • RikkiOpfer Whitney • RikkiSteele-Magee Victoria • RileyBraunstein Jonathan • RileyJohnson Grace • RileyMasters Maddison • RileyPinkerton Courtney • RimaBoujaoude Rana • RimshaAziz Duncan • RinelleWong Vicky • RisaLilly Michael • Risa'Rawrz'Lilly Michael • RiselleSilva Jireh • Rissa Nicholson • RissaAumada Ronnie • RissaNicholson Bill • RitaChang Linda • RitaZhou Pei • RitikMalhotra Priyanka • RiyaGehlot Kevin • RizaHarada Jayson • RizaJao Emma • RizkiSaid Karim • RjAbreo Lena • RobbieRobster Lun • RobbieWightwick book • RobbieWilliford Buggy • RobertaGibson Fernando • RobertFickenscher Charles • RobertLopez Allison • RobertMcIntosh Everyone • RobertoRivera • RobertRaso Devon • RobHuot Susan • RobinBucci Emma • RobinhNguyen Emily • RobinJacobs Gina • RobinLange Ingrid • RobNguyen Rob • RobRowe Brittney • RobynAntoniaaCritcher Corey • RobynCritcher Corey • RobynGreen Stan • RobynRazook Square • RobynRoberts Kay • RobynWeintraub Travis • RochelleKropveld mason • RochelleNeuman Shannon • RochelleSedara Rosie • Rochelle?????Kropveld friend • RochellThompson Cassie • RocioSuikkanen Joanna • RoderichEdelstein Gilbert • RodianneBugeja Larissa • RodolfoSoto Rafael • RohanSmith Nikita • RoishinByrne Elissa • RolandoRodriguez Caitlynn • RolandRoberge Kelsey • RonaldKem Kirsten • RoniLubofsky Margaret • RoniPhillips Alex • RonnieAichroth Julie • RonnieFinley Melanie • RosÃ©Carrillo Tyleah • RosaHernandez Lila • RosalieBerger John • RosalindScoular Audrey • RosalynRico Aeri • RosangelaViana Taylor • RoseanneBowes Martha • RoseCasey Adam • RoseCordell Hunter • RoseCuniglio Carianne • RoseCuniglio Carianne • RoseliaRose bffs • RosemaryFlorido Raphie • RoseMatatix Tim • RosePetal Isra • RosesheskaSchwartz Diana • RosieGrable Kelli • RosieHodsdon Alice • RosieYoung Maddie • RosyBloom Family • Rowan Steve'Priest • RowanaMohamed Amanda • RowanGoodman Maddison • RowanOverwater Glenys • RowanPriest Arran • RowanWhite Alastar • RoxannaQuinn Kelsey • RoxanneMeyer Mallory • RoxanneTan Jane • RoxieCampbell My • RoxyRosario Zach • RozeeRossi Victoria • RozeR Dave • RubaKhalaf Rana • RubanDani Jerry • RubyBilbao Virginia • RubyHarris Jodi • RubyHerbert Lily • RubySzpeflicki Stephen • RuchikaGothoskar Archana • RudhayainiM Juno • RuNay Rukaya • RunaZaman You • RupinderBains Melanie • RussellLau yan • RustiHill Kane • RuthiePina Alice • RutuparnaDas Rtapalli • RyanBagley Aimee • RyanBegen Amy • RyanChandler Shaycarl • RyanCook Larry • RyanDang Renee • RyanFriend Francesca • RyanGreen Samantha • RyanHabiger Alicia • RyanHall Yasmine • RyanJaegerOwen Cassidy • RyanMcKenna Kyle • RyanMolen Rowena • RyanPierce • RyanStandbridge Chloe • RyleyAnderson My • RyuzakiKun Claire • S.K.Miller Molly • SaaraHannan Mother • SaaraJalkanen Marja • SabhaRafiq Masam • SabrieReid Richered • SabrinaButler Gwendolyn • SabrinaGroves Dan • SabrinaHoward Aleena • SabrinaJohnson Loren • SabrinaKelly James • SabrinaLow Sylvia • SabrinaNewsom family • SabrinaQuan Martin • SabrinaRios Daniel • SabrinaSamol Megan • SabrinaWilliams Jeffrey • SabrinaWilliams Steve • SachiPerera Niki • SadeAyinde-Djan Suzanna • SadeenBogari Khoulod • SadieBlouin Stephanie • SadieJ Drew • SadieJane Katie • SadieKratzer Nathan • SadiePetitt Becca • SadikaAhmad Iskander • SafwaanZamakda Chazia • SahilNirula Amrita • SaigeLove Mola • SaiS Sriram • SajreenaFern Praky • SakoSerberus Andrew • SalmaCalito Kimberly • SalmaNasr Mona • SamanjarZ Zain • SamanthaAdair • SamanthaAlley Kaitlin • SamanthaBeard Cindi • SamanthaBergonia Jerimiah • SamanthaBraver Oreo • SamanthaBray Bailey • SamanthaBrockett Donna • SamanthaBrooke Carmody • SamanthaCastaneda Galaxy • SamanthaCelestino Kory • SamanthaCole Daniel • SamanthaCorbin Deborah • SamanthaCortès Dasha • SamanthaCullers Sam • SamanthaDenison My • SamanthaDixon Krista • SamanthaFisher Jarrod • SamanthaHinrichs Steven • SamanthaHitchcock Baylee • SamanthaHoeben Cindy • SamanthaHupp Jaime • SamanthaJohnson Laura • SamanthaJones Ross • SamanthaLangenkamp Jelani • SamanthaLaureenCole Daniel • SamanthaLively Emily • SamanthaMarshall Vickie • SamanthaMason Yvonne • SamanthaMassie Matthew • SamanthaMilner Carly • SamanthaNelson Jesse • SamanthaOehley Barack • SamanthaOng Jeffrey • SamanthaPerry Morgan • SamanthaPersaud Chaz • Samantha Purpalducks • SamanthaRoberts Clarks • SamanthaRobertson Samantha • SamanthaSalazar Amanda • SamanthaSanderson Josh • SamanthaSarmiento Rachelle • SamanthaSedge Jessica • SamanthaSibrava Jimmy • SamanthaSievert Ricardo • SamanthaSinclair Kiera • SamanthaSturges Neil • SamanthaTan Avalon • SamanthaToney Leslie • SamanthaTongue ROB • SamanthaToriJohnson Laura • SamanthaVernon Kayla • SamanthaWhite Madison • SamanthaWhiting Maryam • SamanthaYoast Adam • SamanthaZiencina Hady • SamanthiaCunningham Samanthia • SamanthiaCunningham Jamie • SamBarkawitz Jaime • SamChoy Shane • SamCiocan Mia • SamEarle Bridgit • SamFinstad Mindy • SamGorham Kyle • SamHalford Louise • SamHelias Elan • SamHill Daniel • SamiBezar Chase • SamiDalzell-Matthew Kate •

SamiL Haylee • SamiMericle Rowling • SamirGhosh Manisha • Sami-semicolonMericle Clare • SamJones Chris • SamLenz Joey •
SamLcan vita • Sammy Jones Zona • SammieEvans Karon • SammieReese James • SammiMicke Bobby • SammiMicke Nada • SammiPaglia Karen •
SammyMay Samantha • SammyLopez Daniel • SammyPollino My • SammyRibble Brandon • SamParadis Chris • SamsonChamson Nilofar • SamsonVentress Sarah •
SamStoves Mitzi • SamSumulong Annette • SamTitus Erica • SamuelBarnes Stephanie • SamuelMorris Samantha • SamVandermeyden Matt • SamWallace Brigid • SamsonMughal Kimberly •
Sanah.livani Lillianne • Sanderder Melissa • SandraBenjamin joshua • SandraChen Steven • SandraLam Alyson • SandraSolis Anse • SandyAllen Abigail • SandyBehre Collin • SandyHanna •
John • SansNguyen Emma • Santiago Venticinque Bethany • SaraBeeke Faziah • SaraBrandonisio Loretta • SaraBuhlaiga GOD • SaraCameron Caleb • SaraChapeli •
Katy • SaraChen Life • SaraDada Zara • SaraGillis Damon • SaraGrassie Severus • SaraGuffer Andrew • SaraHAgnew Kelby • SaraHAleyshaJabir Rowinza • SaraHChua Jennifer •
SaraHBeason Anderson Alv • SaraHBannan Jennet • SaraHBatman kassi • SaraHBieber Nancy • SaraHBoden Nathan • SaraHBradley Hollie •
SaraHBosse-Chaseton James • SaraDe Brea • SaraHDeryio Erin • SaraHDias Lupe • SaraHDixon Wallace • SaraHDorÂ©A Mo • SaraHCastro Drew • SaraHChau Vera • SaraHChristoff Scott • SaraHChua Jennifer •
SaraHDavison James • SaraHDe Brea • SaraHDeryio Erin • SaraHDias Lupe • SaraHGolden Lynch • SaraHGaskill Jesus • SaraHHadley Sophie • SaraHHammond friend • SaraHHarbey father •
SaraHEmily Katnlss • SaraHColemand Elijah • SaraHCorn Stefan • SaraHFalk Donald • SaraHEvans Melanie • SaraHFaulkner Matthew • SaraHFlores Jesse • SaraHFreaken Murray •
Stephan • SaraHFugate Maureen • SaraHGabriella Chris • SaraHHernandez Haylin • SaraHHogg Jacob • SaraHHorgan God • SaraHHousley Tracey • SaraHarahim Alicia • SaraHighdal John •
SaraHJabir Rowinza • Sarah-Jane Dale • SaraHMarie Austin • SaraHLevi Vincent • SaraHLewites Tam • SaraHJobe Kailani • SaraHJohnson Felix • SaraHJordan Kristy • Sarah-JoyWickes Michael • SaraHKelley •
Colby • SaraHLacatus Johnny • SaraHLang Cymric • SaraHLevine Caitlin • SaraHMax Chelsea • SaraHMc Lauren • SaraHMcCabe My • SaraHMcGibbon Ashley • SaraHMelancon Christine •
Myriah • SaraHMargason Alex • SaraHMarie Austin • SaraHMarieSchwomeyer Haley • SaraHNastiti Arfidiata • SaraHNelson Betty • SaraHNewhall Nancy • SaraHNicole Stephan •
SayonSisay Emily • ScarletMarks Kyle • ScarletManson Jeneth • ScottBiddle Jackie • ScottMartinkus Alberta • ScottMaxwell Lisa • ScottPanda Nikki • ScottSiller Deborah • ScottWludther •
Kathryn • SeanBlanchard Ella • SeanAntill Katina • SeanEng Jasmine • SeanLake Hannah • SeanMay Spencer • SeanO'Neill Stephanie • SeanRodgers My • SeanSalas Jo • SeanStudd •
Keith • SaraHSmith Brian • SaraHSvoboda David • SaraHTady Amy • SaraHTahar Alicia • SaraHTeresa Everyone • SaraHSirker Jessica • SaraHSisters-Smith Sisters • SaraHSmiddy Danielle •
Olivia • SerenaLugo Jacob • SerenaMaree Logan • SerenaMusser Alvin • SerenaPattan Edith • SerenMarkovich Determined • SethMischo Noreen • SeyChan Danny •
SeyiAkinwale Stella • ShaCollado family • ShaePirrone Steven • ShafiLotfi My • SetHolland Hannah • SerenaLily • SerenaJones Lily • SerenaLugo •
Amanda • ShanaDehoyos diego • ShantaBecke Aditi • ShaniRiley Bela • ShandyVinian Erin • ShanmaLowe Matt • ShannonArmwine Lexi • ShannonBowden Shannon • SeyChan Danny •
Christopher • ShannonCampbell Sydney • ShannonClarke Aditi • ShannonHardy Deborah • ShannonGladden Elizabeth • ShannonGemma Elizabeth • ShannonGladden •
Doug • ShannonMassey Karen • ShannonMcCadyean Joanne • ShannonMcFadyean Joanne • ShannonPayne Vera • ShannonPelzer Andrew • ShevnLam •
Vanessa • ShannonPrendergast Haya • ShannonSanderson Deb • ShannonSheppard Maria • ShannonSutter Marion • ShannonTroy Larry • SharlysaBrown •
Josh • SharonZamora Karyna • SharonZhu Ashley • ShawnLaskowski frankie • ShawnaClark Jessica • ShawnO'Donnell Keauna • ShannonGuild Jadon • ShawnaRobinson •
Britt • ShawneeBowman Kylie • Shawn-LaskiClarke • ShayJenna Hayley • SheaCada Kathleen • SheaWood anthony • SheikhakPauline •
ShaynaLewis Cassandra • ShaynaQuigley Emilia • SheilaCampos Steven • ShelbyRoger • ShelbyFuller Craig • ShelbyLarva Wendy • ShelbyLynnWidener Laurie •
SheilaClark Patricia • ShelbyWayward-Castor Emily • ShelbyHughes Erin • ShelbyParrish Kenneth • ShelbyPersons Steven • ShelbyRosli Dorothy • ShelbySmith Mandee •
melissa • ShelbyDowne Emma • ShelbyDuran josh • ShelbyFlenady Darryl • ShelbyWidener melissa • ShelbyWilliams Shelby • ShelbyWinchester ALEX • SheilaAdao Keith •
Andrew • ShelbyMcGraw Society • ShelbyvandenBurg Ian • ShelbyNichols Kenneth • SheonaAnnaAnja Krish • SheridanBades Mary • SherifaHafez Nour • SherilynTan •
Phillipe • SheriStirling Seth • SheryHy Sherly • SherlynBryne Gelz • SheryCo Tony • SherryLam-Wong Andy • SherriLynn William • ShewinChen Jessica • ShevonLam •
Derek • SheyaMahmood Nisha • SheilaLinasan Canson • SheilaVallente Kim • ShirinZaidi Shuja • ShirleyLang Abigail • ShirleyStensberg Mike • ShivangiSharma •
Taylor • ShrutiChotikar Anaika • ShrineBrown Skandar • SophiLogeswaran Hiren • SophSaraoshi Chelyn • SophMccarthy shane • SpazKostyal My • SpencerBajicar My • SpencerWoolard Friends •
SreyaPokkali Ella • SrishtiSharma Sanjay • StaasJim Rachel • StaceeHush Edward • StaceyCox Alex • StaceyLynn Snyder • StaceyTurner Maxine • StacieMartinez •
Gavin • StacieThomas Stephen • StaciKeith Jerry • StacyBlack Jade • StacyBurkhater Sally • StacyJackson Steven • StaelFisher Emma • StaceMeadows Michael •
StellaDryhurst mom • StellaGrace Julia • StellaSo Christina • StephanieRice Tyler • StephanieBetters Val • StephanieBranco grandma • StephanieBroerjes Vic • StephanieBrown Ryan •
Joseph • StephanieEdens Merena • StephanieCapps Riley • StephanieClick allison • StephanieColvin Bill • StephanieCortner The • StephanieCuccio •
Sophie • StephanieCalhoun Marc • StephanieCardona Nina • StephanieChan Jacky • StephanieGarcia Ozzie • StephanieGirl Orin • StephanieGolphin Mariann •
Fatima • SkylerLara Chris • SofiaBennettRose Menroth • SkylerHasley Melissa • SiraMohammed Rebecca • SkylaWorth Daniel • SkylaLilly Love • SkylarKeogh Cyann • SkyLeBeau •
Gina • SitaraTilly David • SitlMckeisam Lolly • StephEllenHutton Matt • StephHutton Matt • StephMagee Jake • StephPenhail Daniel • StephRukavina evan • Steph Smoluk •
Victor • StephanieMerhai Jalyn • StephanieNeff Daniel • StephanieNugent Brook • StevePenhail Daniel • StephRoberts Jackie • StephRukavina evan • StephWood friends •
Family • StephanieRaines Jack • StephanieRivas Isabel • StephanieRivera My • StephanieSammon Marianne • StephanieWoehl Meena • StevenMariani Shane • SummerHundleyy Jesse •
StephanieWatkins Caitlin • StephanieWei Jennifer • StephanieZuniga Nella • StephanieZwolenik Dawn • StephanieJefferies Madison • StephenMcGhee Elaina • StephenThorpe Todd •
GOD • Steph?Penhall daniel • SteveEinhorn Megan • StevenCooper Trinnay • StevenWhite Austin • StuartMann Julie • SudhadraVemuri mom • SueSoud wow • SukhiChuhan Inderjeet •
SteveWillywag Steve • StevieNoesel Stevie • Su-KimMacdonald Severn • SunaiaBelikov Renee • SusanCarrTrish • SumerBel Breanna • SummerDee Jake • SummerHundley Jesse •
SummerTwiztidNative Raven • SummerVogel David • SunnnraÂ©Calvin • SunainaPerera Sonali • SunenaKara Rajvinder • SunnieDeupree Leslie • SunnyAdriana Amber • Sunnyde Michelle •
SurajGopie Travis • SureshFajardo Frank • SusanBelikov Renee • SusanCarr Trish • SusanGarland Oris • SusanHuynh Albert •

My Dearest Dana,

In being the greatest teammate, my best friend, my faithful guardian, my blue-eyed angel, my sister, and my love, you give me hope. Words cannot describe how you have changed me, nor can they describe what you mean to me. Thank you for always being there for me, for always crying with me, for always laughing with me, and for always loving me. Happy 18th Birthday love! May all your wishes come true and your life be filled with hope, happiness, and love

Yours Always,
Laura

# Photo Credits

Photographs are from bigstockphoto.com unless otherwise noted.

p. 9: © Kobyakov
p. 10: © Nolte
p. 11: © Paha_L
p. 12: © Linnea
p. 13: © Perrush
p. 14: © diego cervop. 15: © AriLeo
p. 16: © fredgoldstein
p. 17: © CleoMiu
p. 18: © karenroach
p. 19: © EastWestImaging
p. 20: © Yuri_Arcurs
p. 21: © jas0420
p. 22: © baileydog
p. 23: © hannamonika
p. 24: © clublavelapc
p. 25: © 4774344sean
p. 26: © Carlush
p. 27: © toxawww
p. 28: girl © Reno12; animals © AlexBannykh
p. 29: © theodor38
p. 30: © denverphotopro
p. 31: background © poofy; people © MaszaS
p. 32: © AndreyStratilatov
p. 33: © ruivalesousa
p. 34: Julijah
p. 35: children © Tina B; adults © Goruppa
p. 36: © chuckee
p. 37: © JANE SEPTEMBER
p. 38: © StephanieFrey
p. 39: © jlern
p. 40: © pkazmercyk
p. 41: © Ronen
p. 42: © Andrushko Galyna
p. 43: © 4774344sean

p. 44: © LmidgitD
p. 45: © songbird839
p. 46: bus © Noot54; girl © Le loft 1911
p. 47: © contas
p. 48: © Olivier
p. 49: © Yuri_Arcurs
p. 50: © webrx
p. 51: © octabas
p. 52: © Paha_L
p. 53: © MaszaS
p. 54: © andres
p. 55: © lisafx
p. 56: © Ni Der Lander
p. 57: © koun
p. 58: © Andrushko Galyna
p. 59: © Otna Ydur
p. 60: © prasanthsukumaran
p. 61: © quayside
p. 62: © olly2
p. 63: window © robcocquyt; landscape © missanzi
p. 64: © alkir
p. 65: © darrenmbaker
p. 66: © MikLav
p. 67: man © Ivonnewierink; background © rgbspace
p. 68: © andres
p. 69: © kjpargeter
p. 70: © barsik
p. 71: balloons © Larsena; couple © warrengoldswain
p. 72: © topcat57
p. 73: parking lot © Karp; man © Paha_L

p. 74: © ratme
p. 75: © Alhovik
p. 76: © smphoto
p. 77: © andres
p. 78: © red2000
p. 79: © lovleah
p. 80: © gvictoria
p. 81: © Pond Shots
p. 82: © Julijah
p. 83: © Yuri_Arcurs
p. 84: © bigstockphoto .com
p. 85: bride © smartfoto; flourish © nicemonkey
p. 86: © pressmaster
p. 87: © Anton Prado PHOTOGRAPHY
p. 88: wings © adroach; musicians © Laures; man © Steve Byland; background © mpemberton
p. 89: © hartphotograher
p. 90: © arekmalang
p. 91: © purplecat
p. 92: © Illustrations by designer (Marisabel)
p. 93: © zach123
p. 94: © Orange Line Media
p. 95: © gareth12468
p. 96: © darrenmbaker
p. 97: couple © iofoto. com; cake © lisafx
p. 98: © chukephoto
p. 99: © dolgachov
p. 100: © og-vision
p. 101: © vladacanon
p. 102: © blas
p. 103: © warren goldswain

p. 104: © Andrushko Galyna
p. 105: photo frame & board © devon; girls © lisafx
p. 106: © MaszaS
p. 107: © barsik
p. 108: © lovleah
p. 109: © keeweeboy
p. 110: © MaszaS
p. 111: © clearviewstock
p. 112: © wrangler
p. 113: © Yuri_Arcurs
p. 114: © bg_knight
p. 115: © arquiplay
p. 116: © Paha_L
p. 117: © dip2000
p. 118: © VeryUnique
p. 119: © barsik
p. 120: © magicinfoto
p. 121: © designer's photo (Jan)
p. 122: © elenathewise
p. 123: © davinci
p. 124: © eric1513
p. 125: © vgstudio
p. 126: © alptraum
p. 127: © Jeanne Hatch
p. 128: © Ximagination
p. 129: © fredgoldstein
p. 130: © monkey businessimages
p. 131: © dolgachov
p. 132: background © Sandralise; chain © Orla
p. 133: © nrubocp. 134: © Forgiss
p. 135: © Joss

# About the Designers

Special thanks to Garrett, Jan, Jana, Linda, Marisabel, Sha, and Xiaodi for their tireless work in bringing this project to its visually stunning conclusion.

 **Garrett:** I'm eternally grateful to Gaby and GivesMeHope for letting me put pictures to someone else's inspiring words. I hope you enjoy this book!

 **Jan:** GMH shows that God is constantly weaving His nifty little miracles into our everyday lives, and proves that there is light in this darkness!

 **Jana:** I'm a 16-year-old college student who aims to give hope to others in her own little ways.

 **Linda:** I am constantly thankful for the love and hope my friends and family share with me, and I'm happy to have been a part of something like GMH.

 **Marisabel:** I'm a self-taught Puerto Rican illustrator and designer. It was a joy to work for such an inspiring project as GMH!

 **Sha:** As a self-taught designer from the Philippines, I loved working with GMH. Beautiful stories. Beautiful idea. This project really GIVES ME HOPE!

 **Xiaodi:** I am a Chinese teenager who started designing at age 11. Working on the GMH book has been great and a dream come true. I <3 TSwift!